CHOREOGRAPHING
THE
STAGE MUSICAL

Choreographing the Stage Musical

MARGOT SUNDERLAND
with
KENNETH PICKERING

Illustrations by Philip Engleheart

J. GARNET MILLER LTD
NEW YORK
THEATRE ARTS BOOKS/ROUTLEDGE

First published in 1989 by
J. GARNET MILLER LTD
311 Worcester Road, Malvern, Worcestershire
© Margot Sunderland and Ken Pickering 1989

First published in the U.S.A. in 1990 by
Theatre Arts Books
an imprint of Routledge
29 West 35th Street
New York, NY 10001
U.S.A.
ISBN 0-87830-029-5 (hard-back)
0-87830-030-9 (paper-back)

British Library Cataloguing in Publication Data
Sunderland, Margot
    Choreographing the stage musical
    I. Choreography
    I. Title II.   Pickering, Kenneth
782.81   GV1782.5

        ISBN 0-85343-586-3

Printed in Great Britain by BPCC Wheatons Ltd, Exeter

Acknowledgement

Sincere thanks to
Jill Methley
for knowledge on musical repertoire

The authors gratefully acknowledge the permission granted by Chappell Music to quote the words of the chorus *Oklahoma*, by Novello & Co Ltd to quote 'Potiphar' from *Joseph and his Amazing Technicolour Dreamcoat*, by Carlin Music Corporation to quote 'Light of the World' from *Godspell* and by Samuel French Ltd to quote the words of the songs 'Come One, Come All' and 'Bingo' from *Beowulf*. The books and the scores for these musicals can be obtained from the publishers.

Contents

CHAPTER	PAGE
Preface	9
Introduction: Including a Glossary of Basic Terms used in the Book	11
1 How and When to Move in Songs	15
2 Choreography for the Accompanying Chorus during the Song or Dance	20
3 General Vocabulary	25
4 Physical Contact	48
5 Groupings and Designs	63
6 Regular Formations	75
7 Dealing with the Co-Existence of Groups	84
8 Transition Techniques	91
9 Using Music and Structuring Time	100
10 The Role of Properties, the Set and Costume in Choreography	108
11 Pre-Planning and Rehearsing Choreography	116
Appendix I	120
Appendix II	151

Preface

Live entertainment which draws on the arts of singing, acting and dancing is almost as old as the theatre itself. In every tradition and culture some form of music-drama has invariably proved to be the most popular type of theatre. In English-speaking countries it is certainly the case today that people who would not normally go to the theatre will turn out to see a musical. This popularity is reflected in the vast sums expended by managements on the lavish staging of musicals in the professional theatre and by the ever-thriving thousands of amateur companies who overcome incredible difficulties to mount their productions. Secondary Schools and Colleges find that the staging of a musical is an ideal way to exploit the vitality of large numbers of students and they usually play to packed houses. Consequently there is now a constant demand for new shows to satisfy every part of the market.

Undoubtedly, one of the reasons for the popularity of the musical is that the cast and audience can take the tunes away with them in their minds. Songs from shows have, in fact, become something of an industry in their own right providing large incomes for record companies and music publishers and, to a lesser extent, for the performers and writers themselves. The involvement of the recording industry in the success of musicals has not only extended the audience well beyond the confines of the theatre but has enabled shows to become known through a single song; it has ensured a far higher standard of presentation at every level and far greater sophistication in orchestration and general musicianship. Audiences, having once heard a first-rate recording by a West End or Broadway cast, are less tolerant of the second-rate.

A more far-reaching effect of the recording industry on the theatre has been the pop music phenomenon of the last twenty-five years.

Rock music with its associated fashions in dress, dance and behaviour, appealing especially to the young, has produced a revolutionary attitude to entertainment. The early heroes of rock 'n' roll made much of their impact in musical films and while this tendency continues to a lesser extent, many rock-stars have become leading performers in the live theatre and have brought a distinctive approach to the modern musical. Theatre choreography has also been changed radically by the influence of the various uninhibited and spontaneous styles of dancing which derive from the whole ethos and atmosphere of pop music and theatre technology has been forced to accommodate the expectations of the rock-concert or 'disco'.

Many directors are relatively confident when handling the dialogue of a musical, they may even be at ease with sung solos, duets or static choruses but the modern musical seems to demand almost constant movement and dance: this is where so many productions founder. Even if a director is able to draw on the services of a specialist choreographer the fact remains that for much of the production *he* is also a choreographer and needs to be aware of all the problems and possibilities of dance.

At this point we should draw attention to the absolute necessity for a sensitive and clearly thought-out working relationship between Director, Choreographer and Musical Director. The Director must have and retain an overall vision but this must be based on a thorough understanding of what the Musical Director wishes to achieve from the score and a deep knowledge of the musical requirements themselves. Likewise, the Choreographer must be intimately acquainted with both the rhythmic and melodic structure of the score and with the dramatic function of the dance routines and must share the aims of both the Director and the musical Director. This does not mean that the Choreographer is passively compliant but must enable his or her colleagues in the direction team to extend their concept of the piece by an appreciation of the choreography. This delicate balance of power can only be achieved if discussions and disputes take place before rehearsals begin; this demands far more careful preparation than many people seem prepared to make but there is nothing more deplorable than a Choreographer or Musical Director drifting into a rehearsal with a few vague ideas that they would like to try out while the cast are steaming with frustration. There is, of course, a place for the 'let's try that and see' approach but it must be clearly agreed with Director and cast that certain numbers would benefit from it. The situation in which members of the direction team disagree in public is to be avoided at all costs and this often means a precise understanding of who is running a particular rehearsal and some tact and restraint from those who are *not*. Every rehearsal schedule should include sufficient time for each of these key figures to achieve their aims in the way which seems best to them.

This book is intended for all those who wish to create that unity between music, language and movement which is capable of generating so much excitement in the live performance of a stage musical. It assumes no previous experience in dance although the book can be used with profit by those dancers who suddenly find themselves in the rôle of stage choreographer. Co-operation between the members of a creative team is essential and we feel, therefore, that this handbook will be equally useful to directors and musical directors and teachers who sometimes have to do it all!

H.M.S.
K.W.P.
Nonington College, 1987

Introduction

Choreography fulfils many roles in a musical. We regard the following as most important:

1. To generate energy
As Kislan states, a musical is 'life-affirming'. Dance can both generate and provide a natural outlet for energy.

2. To express moods and heighten feeling states
In ways unavailable to the dialogue: many moods and feelings are more readily expressed through movement than through any other medium.

3. To complement other media
Dance can draw attention to rhythms in the music - thus a rhythm can be experienced visually, kinetically and aurally. It can also complement lyrics through the use of illustrative gesture. Dance, therefore, can ensure that the integral subtleties of the other media used in musicals are more noticeable.

4. To change atmosphere
A change of atmosphere or mood is in fact a change in energy level. It can often be conveyed with more impact and more immediately through movement than through dialogue.

5. To bring out humour
Visual wit can often cause much energetic laughter. It is the humour of the visual contradiction, a sad face with a happy body; imitation; the odd one out; the ridiculous contortion; the unusual physical contact between two people or a group, the idiosyncratic gesture; the danced mannerism.

6. To entertain

7. To add spectacle

8. To display costume

9. To further relationships

10. To colour characterisation

11. To convey physical states such as forms of aggression and affection

12. To display ritual and celebration

13. To manipulate time: accelerate it or slow it down or suspend it

14. To heighten suspense

15. To portray fantasy and fantasy worlds such as dreams, the unconscious

16. To further the plot

The Distinguishing Features of Choeography for Musicals

Generally speaking dance for musicals needs to have *pace*, *rhythm* and *drive*. It must be neat and produce clear designs. It must be precise both temporally and spatially. The movement vocabulary can be very varied stylistically but it is limited by the need to leave sufficient breath to sing loudly! Movement must not restrict the vocal chords.

There can be less complex choreographic development than with other forms of theatre dance because the dance in musicals has to cope with the many changes, interruptions and transitions into songs or dialogue and the spectator needs to divide his attention between the auditory and the visual, occurring simultaneously.

A GLOSSARY OF BASIC CHOREOGRAPHIC TERMS USED IN THIS BOOK

Before examining the various possibilities of choreography in the musical, we must define a number of terms frequently used by choreographers to describe their work.

Canon

A term borrowed from music which means a single movement or phrase sequence of movements performed by one dancer which is then repeated by one or more other dancers. This can happen after the first person has completed the movement or during it. The latter use of canon is sometimes known as ripple canon, where there is an overlap of movements and the repeats occur with a fast tempo. A 'ripple canoned' phrase therefore appears to gather energy and sometimes acceleration throughout its duration.

Concertina Effect

This occurs when the distance between members of a group closes. A concertina effect is sometimes the unfortunate result of a supposedly equidistant group whilst travelling. One member may catch up with another member. The group will, therefore, lose their state of equidistance.

Dosy-Do

A folk dance term. Partners face each other, walk towards each other and pass back to back (passing right or left shoulders) and finally walk backwards to their original starting places.

Dynamics

The strength or energy of a movement, e.g. as in the differing emphasis or intensity of a movement.

Equidistant Grouping

Grouping where distance between each group member is the same. The result is often a tidy formal group. Equidistant grouping is often known as a FORMATION, particularly if the group dance in unison.

Freeze

A movement which is held for a certain length of time so that there is a pause in the dance, a section of stillness.

Gesture

A movement of a limb which makes no contact with the floor for support. A gesture is, therefore, differentiated from the step.

Illustrative Gesture

A movement which illustrates, or in some way refers to, words or a word in the lyrics of a song.

Isolation

A movement which involves placing one particular body part out of its usual position so that the effect is to isolate it from the rest of the dancer's body and therefore to draw attention to it. Many isolated movements (e.g. knee isolation, shoulder isolation, head isolation) are effective whilst the rest of the body is motionless.

Level

The quality of space which is concerned with the height at which movement takes place, e.g. low level - normal standing position; high level -heels off the floor, standing on tiptoe.

Masking (or Blocking)

Where one or more dancers stand too near to or actually in front of other dancers so that dancers are wholly or partially hidden from some or all of the spectators for some or all of the time.

Pas de Bourrée

A frequently used 'running' step, usually comprising three steps (right left right or left right left) performed over two beats in time. The three steps can be, for example:
step behind, side, in front or front, side, behind. (r) (l) (r) (l) (r) (l)

Peripheral Movement or Gesture

A movement which is performed when limbs are out-stretched, thus performed on the periphery of the body as opposed to near the body centre (central movement).

Polish

A term meaning to rehearse a movement sequence of an individual dancer or group of dancers; being very exacting, clarifying and correcting the smallest detail of a movement (e.g. Where are you looking? Are your hands facing up to the ceiling or downwards? How far are your feet apart?)

Symmetrical Movement

Where each side of the body is identical.

Syncopation

An effect whereby the stress patterns of an expected rhythm are disturbed - so there is an accenting of usually unaccented beats and a missing of beats.

Tempo

A term borrowed from music. The speed or pace of a movement phrase or dance.

Transition (Movement)

A movement or set of movements whose purpose is to act as a bridge between two different movement events, themes or phrases.

A movement transition can also refer to a connecting or linking dance between the different media in a musical, e.g. dialogue, DANCE, song.

Travelling

A movement or movements which move across the floor as opposed to staying on the spot.

Unison

A dance, a movement phrase or a single movement where more than one person dances at the same time with identical movements.

Vibratory Movement

A sort of movement typified by continual bursts of vibrating movement.

Visual Lines

A term applied to an occasion where a performer looks in a certain direction and a spectator follows his gaze.

Vocabulary

The content of a dance, the steps, the gestures, the actual movements which it is comprises.

1. How and when to move in songs

Deciding Whether or Not to Dance a Song

Having read through a text and score, it is not always obvious whether or not to dance a certain song. It is always important, however, to question the justification for each inclusion of a danced number in the musical. For indeed one can 'over-dance' a musical. This becomes apparent when the plot seems secondary or is even lost sight of to some extent, due to the dance taking up too much of the time. This may be because too many numbers are being danced or because the numbers themselves are too long. Indeed a major problem with the musical is how to share the time available between dialogue, song, music and dance.

First, it is important to identify the obvious 'excuses' and places for dance. This is particularly easy in musicals which include in the scenario a built-in dance event. The following musicals are examples where this is the case:

Cabaret - dance in a night club
My Fair Lady - ball scene
Grease - dance contest
Easter Parade, *Cover Girl* and *A Chorus Line* -all about chorus girls
Saturday Night Fever - disco contest
Blue Skies - about a Broadway dancing star
West Side Story - dance
Rocky Horror Show - celebration dance
Seven Brides for Seven Brothers - dance
The Band Wagon and *All That Jazz* - both about a Broadway show

It is also easy where the very plot itself is about dance, for example, *Chorus Line* or *All That Jazz*. Secondly, look carefully at the script and score to see what other roles and uses dance may offer. Remember those qualities which dance can bring to a show as outlined in our Introduction. Then in considering whether dance could help in any of these ways, study carefully the content of each song and its position in the show. It may be possible, for example, to foresee that after a ballad song followed by a long dialogue section, there is likely to be a worrying loss of pace and momentum, coupled with a drop in the energy level. This may be restored to the optimum level through using dance. As well as reading the lyrics, listen to the music of a number with a view to the possible merit of extra emphasis through dance. Consider whether movement could happily co-exist with that piece of music and those lyrics, would dance be a strengthening addition or just a distraction to either or both? Would a static grouping or purely gestured accompaniment be more appropriate?

It is difficult to generalise over these matters, although there are some general guidelines. There are certain points in musicals where it is often wise to exploit the energy dance can supply. The opening number and numbers at the beginning of Acts II and III are particular examples of this. Dance in the opening number of Act II can also act as a re-statement or reminder of the atmosphere before the curtain dropped. Dance has also an important role to play in the production number, which is usually an event where everything is at its height. The stage is full, the music loud and there is lots of energy. Moreover, dance can bring out the humour in a comic number through such devices as imitation; unison movement; odd use of isolated body parts; hiccuping syncopation and exaggerated mannerisms. The ballad and the songs with slower tempos on the other hand are often unsuited to choreography. When dancers try to parallel the gentle flowing qualities in slow tempoed music, the choreography often deteriorates into a combination of over indulgent arm gesturing and sloppy spatial positions. This can only degrade the music and reduce the number to a state of slushy sentimentality. Similarly very fast tempoed numbers do not lend themselves easily to dance. Words and music can 'travel' faster than movement. Movement that fails to keep up with the tempo of sung lyrics is both farcical and embarassing. With the patter song, for example, dance would only detract from the brilliance of the rapid speed and succinct staccato nature of the spoken or sung lyrics. The patter song is primarily an auditory experience and should be presented as such. Any 'visual' additions in terms of movement should be minor, small hand gestures or an occasional little step for example.

Gesture for The Singer

People are accustomed to fidgeting and touching their own bodies in a whole manner of ways whilst talking. They can often feel denuded if asked to stand motionless for any length of time. Gesturing during a song, therefore, often provides the singer with a release for tension, a feeling of confidence and a sense of movement. Gesturing prevents singers adopting a militaristic stance or 'stuffed dummy' look which often arise from the tensions and self-consciousness over the problem of 'what do I do with my hands?'. If, however, it is important for some reason that the singer holds his arms still for a long time, he may feel more at ease by holding both hands in front of the body as shown in Figure 1. Arms held by the sides often look both unnatural and uncomfortable.

The chosen performer of the song can take some responsibility for the gesture he uses by experimenting with what feels comfortable. This is often more effective than the choreographer trying to impose gestures which are simply not natural to that performer. Naturally this does not prevent the choreographer from intervening if there is some inappropriate or over use of gesturing.

Illustrative and Literal Gesture

Gesture can be used to emphasise or draw attention to lyrics. It can be a way of ensuring that the spectator takes notice of the words. It is almost as if though they are spoken twice - verbally and physically. 'Illustrative gesture' refers to literal gesture usually of the hands and arms (but not exclusively so) which imitates concrete and abstract nouns and verbs in the lyrics. It is usually the nouns and verbs lending themselves most easily to visual and kinetic imagery which are selected by the choreographer for this purpose. Some songs

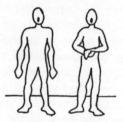

Figure 1

offer more opportunities for illustrative gesture than others. Obviously songs referring mainly to abstract concepts, for example the economy, efficiency, pragmatism, are unsuitable. Moreover, the imitative aspect of illustrative gesture lends itself more readily to humorous or light hearted songs, such as 'Everybody Ought to Have a Maid' (*A Funny Thing Happened on the Way to the Forum*) or 'Brush Up Your Shakespeare' (*Kiss Me Kate*) as opposed to ones with more serious overtones such as 'Some Enchanted Evening' and 'Bally High' (*South Pacific*); 'If ever I would leave you' (*Camelot*) and 'Don't Cry for Me Argentina' (*Evita*). Miming concrete nouns (for example teapot, toothbrush) is often more comical than miming verbs (for example drop, rise), as dance is plainly a more natural habitat for the latter.

Generally, it would be overdone for a whole song to depend entirely on a succession of illustrative gestures without the supplement of more abstract movements in parts. If too many words in close proximity are illustrated in movement, not only is the result likely to be farcical but it may also detract, ironically enough, from the spectator's concentration on the meaning of the lyrics. He may 'over attend' to the visual. Moreover, illustrative gesture happily exists combined and interchanged with abstract movement in a song, for example one word illustrative, the next not, the first three lines illustrative and the whole of the next verse not.

Illustrative gesture can be attractive both in an equidistant symmetrical formation and in a more naturalistic grouping. It is also attractive to have different groups together on stage, some of which are performing abstract dance movements, whilst others are using illustrative gesture. Similarly, co-existing groups, all using illustrative gesture but with different 'illustrations' can have great visual appeal. In the polite tea-drinking scene in Figure 2, as may be found in 'Tea for Two' (*No No Nanette*) for example, all three groups A, B and C have different tea-drinking gestures. This same device for co-existing groups could be used for 'putting-on-make-up' scenes, (e.g. 'One Halloween' from *Applause*); 'chatting-at-a-party' scenes (e.g. 'Backstage Babble' from *Applause*) or 'trying-on-a-hat' scenes (e.g. 'I'm So Pretty' from *West Side Story* or 'Ribbons Down My Back' from *Hello Dolly*.)

A dance can be loosely as opposed to directly or specifically illustrative of the lyrics. That is it may include literal gesture relevant to whole sentences, verses or even to the overall theme of the song as opposed to certain specific words. The line 'I'm doing the housework' for example, could be illustrated in movement by several exaggerated mime gestures suggesting hoovering and ironing, whilst a verse referring to getting up in the morning could be danced by some people brushing their teeth and others frying an egg. A song about sport and exercise, for example 'Fitness Freaks' (*Mothers and Daughters*), could be translated into dance by different groups simulating swimming, jogging, yoga, aerobics etc.

Even more generalised gestures can be used. One hand opening and closing, for example, or a hand gesturing towards the audience in some way may simply convey that the singer is feeling strongly about something at that moment in time. A whole wealth of these more abstract expressive gestures can be gained merely by watching people in conversation in any social situation. Watch their hands particularly.

In using illustrative literal or more abstract gesture in any choreographed context, there are some important rules to observe:

Exaggeration

Perform the gesture far bigger than in everyday life, otherwise the movement may provoke the same frustration as if actors were talking in inaudible tones or it may simply be misinterpreted as fidgeting.

Rhythmical Structure

Give the gesture or sequence of gestures a clear rhythmical phrase. Using a syncopated rhythm for illustrative gesture is often very appealing.

Whole Body Involvement

Do not limit the movement to the arm or hand only. Involve the whole body in the gesture even if only slightly. A torso lean, a step forward, or a bending of the knees, for example, can prevent gestures from looking wooden and unnatural.

Sharp Finish

There is nothing worse than a literal gesture which is sloppy and ill-defined so that it becomes difficult to work out what it is supposed to represent. Give each gesture a staccato full stop, a sharp, crisp finish!

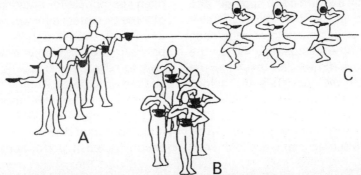

Figure 2

Avoid Clichéd Illustrative Gesture

For example, hand on the heart for sadness, hand on the forehead for worry, saluting.

If the above points are not observed, literal gesture can quickly deteriorate into mime, with a low energy level, rather than dance. If this happens it is likely to be far less attractive as well as losing its novelty value.

Gestures and Movement for the Solo Song

It is often more appropriate for the performer singing a solo number simply to stand still. The solo number sometimes warrants a concentration on the auditory. It can also provide the spectator with a rest from danced movement for a while. Some solo songs, however, include orchestral sections, for example 'Joanna' (*Sweeney Todd*). These are often 32 bars long. Here attention can be transferred somewhat to the movement of the performer. If he is not a particularly talented dancer it is usually better for him merely to walk around during this. A badly danced orchestral section will tend to hamper the effect and professionalism of the good singing that went before. If, on the other hand, the performer can dance, he may use the orchestral section as an opportunity to generate extra energy by performing dance of high technical proficiency covering a lot of space with many peripheral movements. This energy will then be carried over into the next outburst of singing. Some songs do not have an orchestral interlude, but include a few notes at the end of a sung phrase before the lyrics begin again. The soloist (untrained or trained!) may casually throw in a few steps here before singing again. In a duo or trio, the steps can be in unison. Alternatively, during the song, the singer may simply perform a few sporadic arm gestures. Whilst singing, the soloist can also walk around the stage, touching or using parts of the set, walking up steps, leaning on the tree, picking up a flower, for example. As regards gestures, on occasions the soloist may wish to hold a gesture for a long time, at other times to drop the gesture immediately after it has been performed. A gesture can be performed after a sentence of lyrics in the few beats before the next word is sung. Many solo singers finish with greater impact using one strong gesture at the end.

Gestures and Movement for Duetto

The Charm Song
(E.g. 'Some Enchanted Evening' (*South Pacific*); 'I know' (*Guys and Dolls*); 'You'll Never Get Away from Me' (*Gipsy*); 'The Marriage Song' (*Beowulf*); 'There's a Place for Us' (*West Side Story*); 'We Kiss in the Shadows' (*The King and I*).

Avoid over indulgent vocabulary and do not use too many gestures otherwise the charm song may deteriorate into a state of slushy sentimentalism. Sometimes it will be more appropriate for the duos to be sung entirely without gesture. A couple may simply sit together on a settee and sing, perhaps with an occasional leaning towards each other but using no specific movement of the arm or hand. At other times it may be that only one performer is using gesture whilst the other maintains his original arm position throughout the song. If the couple are sitting or standing side by side in danced or gestured song, try to avoid unnatural cranings of the neck which may occur if the couple look over their shoulders in order to communicate. It is quite acceptable for both partners to look straight forwards for most of the time, even if they are engaged in a sung conversation. During a duo, one of the couple may walk away and stand singing to the audience from the front of the stage.

The Art of 'Dancing' Songs

More energetic movement than gesturing is often appropriate for numbers sung by groups of three or more. Common problems encountered with this are how to share breath between the singing and the dancing and how to have both energetic dancing and an audible volume of singing. One solution of course is to supplement the vocals by people singing in the wings. When choreographing, remember that the vocal chords must be unconstricted if performers are required to sing and dance simultaneously. Movements where the head is thrown through the legs, for example, or thrown back, tend to constrict the neck muscles. Similarly, in order to achieve the optimum level of projection, the dancer who is singing should face the audience for much of the time. If there are dancing singers and stationary singers on stage simultaneously, volume may be increased by raising the singers above the dancers on rostra, etc.

The Structure of the Song Paralleled in Dance

The structure of the song can be echoed by that of the dance. For example the refrain in the song may be emphasised by a repeated main motif in the dance. Verse and chorus may be matched by an 'AB CB DB EB' form in the dance. Using a repeated movement sequence for the chorus of perhaps less technical complexity, but with more symmetry, more illustrative gesture than the verse, can complement the comparative simplicity of the lyrics in the chorus of the song.

2. Choreography for the accompanying chorus during the song or dance

The Chorus

This section considers what the chorus can do whilst singing or listening to a song, and dancing or watching dance. Obviously there is a whole range of activities, from the stationary tableau with its natural stance, to the held pose, to the presence of a little movement in the form of a sway or change of weight from one foot to another for example. In many ways a large group of people generate energy simply through their presence. Consequently smaller, more controlled movements which may often seem lacking in energy for a smaller group, can be highly appropriate for a chorus group, doubly so of course if the group is so large that the stage is full. If larger abstract movements are chosen in these circumstances, select 'space saving' vocabulary for example 'in-front-of-the-body-designs'

Standing Still and the Stationary Tableau

The upright and symmetrical stance is often a wise choice for the stationary tableau. It can in fact be visually very powerful for a group to stand absolutely still and sing. It often gives an air of confidence and strength as well as looking tidy! Such stillness is particularly appropriate for some finale numbers where a state of resolution and calm has been reached as for example in the song 'Rose's Turn' (*Gypsy*), or 'Something Wonderful' (*The King and I*), and therefore no 'inner disturbance' needs to be expressed through the arm or hand gesture. It can sometimes look tense and unnatural for a group of singers to place their arms by their sides for these numbers. Placing the arms behind the back or in front is often more

appropriate. If character portrayal is important, add some slight decoration to the stance, one hand cupped in the other for prim ladies, as in songs like 'Every Day a Little Death' (*A Little Night Music*) and 'Elegance' (*Hello Dolly*) for example, or hands in braces for workmen or dockers as in songs like 'Cockney Sparrows' (*The Matchgirls*) and 'With a little bit of luck' (*My Fair Lady*).

If the choreographer does choose this motionless posing for a singing chorus, it is often pleasing for the singers to move on the very last note of the song. This will not seem out of place juxtaposed to the previous stillness. One small staccato gesture with both hands for example is often highly effective as the finish. It helps to establish the end point and fuel it with a sudden burst of energy.

Ways a Silent Chorus can Watch and Listen to Soloist Singers and Dancers

Consider the relationship which the silent chorus group has to the other events on stage at the time. Sometimes they may listen to a soloist singing whilst sitting with a common formal body design in unison groups, as could be used in the song 'Here I am' (*Smike*), or they may sit as individuals, by themselves, in naturalistic positions which would be appropriate when the chorus listen to the minstrel singing 'Long Long Ago' in *Beowulf* for example. At other times they may walk about whilst listening and watching to sustain a previous level of energy. This is demonstrated in Figure 1(a) where the chorus meander behind a danced duo and 1(b) where the chorus follow the soloist around keeping to her side. If a chorus group is stationary and is watching other

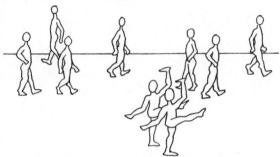

Figure 1(a)

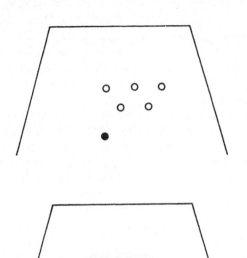

Figure 1(b)

used in isolation, in other words if the body keeps its original directional facing and only the head turns to look at the action. Alternatively, a chorus group may lean diagonally forward with their torsos to stare at what is going on, as could be used for the Ascot scene in *My Fair Lady*.

Commenting on the Action

If the chorus is to comment on an event or happening, use exaggerated rhythmical structure when gesturing. An expression of horror as for example in 'Tevye's Dream' (*Fiddler on the Roof*), could be portrayed with a violent shaking of the wrists set to a syncopated rhythm.

The Silent Chorus as a Moving Backcloth in the Song

The chorus can provide a moving backcloth for the soloists. During a sung duo for example the chorus members may walk across the stage, exit, and then return and repeat. This can provide a delightful contrast, the two people standing still and talking on the pavement, with an endless flow of 'uninvolved' traffic behind them. In Figure 2 the couple sing motionless whilst the chorus leap on and off the stage behind them producing a delightful contrast of speed and energy. (Be aware of the possibility of inappropriate humour in this).

people moving on stage, it is sometimes necessary to accentuate the head movements. Visual lines taken from eye movements of the chorus may be missed completely if the on going action is particularly gripping. Head movements when used to draw attention to visual lines are particularly effective if people are crossing in front of the chorus. If a couple, for example, perform a series of turns from stage right to stage left in ripple canon, the chorus can turn their heads one by one to watch when the couple passes them. Head movements can be more readily noticeable if

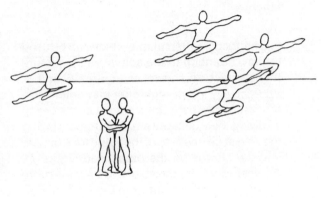

Figure 2

The Chorus Focusing Attention on the Soloists

Members of a chorus can actively help to focus attention on a soloist singer or dancer which can ensure against their becoming a possible distraction. Sometimes this can be achieved by contrast. The soloist, for example, can become part of a group whilst remaining in another sense distinguishable from it. The difference should be clearly marked by costume or stature or sex, for example, to prevent any momentary lapses into merger with the group. In Figure 3 the soloist looks as if she has just forgotten to put on her skirt and in Figure 4 the

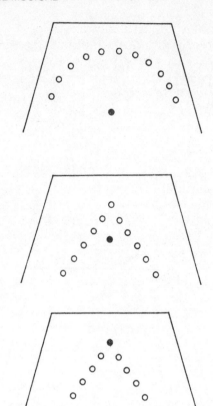

Figure 5

Figure 3

soloist who has only one arm different, merges in too much with the rest of the group.

Figure 4

Figure 6

One 'focusing' technique which can be used to draw attention to the soloist, is the picture frame effect as shown in Figures 5 and 6. Alternatively a choreographer may emphasise the distinction between a soloist and a group by giving them different areas on stage, placing the soloist on one side of the stage for example and the chorus on the other (see Figure 7). Another way is for the soloist to become more overtly 'the odd one out' as in Figure 8, or as in Figure 9 where chorus members in the line perform wildly asymmetric movements and

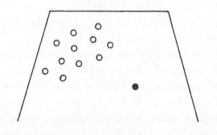

Figure 7

the soloist just stands and sings! Finally it is possible to draw attention by using asymmetry as demonstrated in Figure 10.

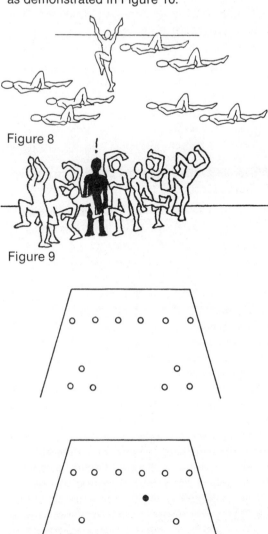

Figure 8

Figure 9

Figure 10

Where to put the Stationary Singing Chorus during the Danced Number

In Figure 11 the singing chorus members are scattered all around the dancing area. This provides a clear framing effect and because of the difference in level, the singers do not interfere with the dancing in any way. Another tidy arrangement is achieved by placing the chorus on either side of the moving group who dance in between them (see Figure 12). This is particularly effective if the dancers in the main

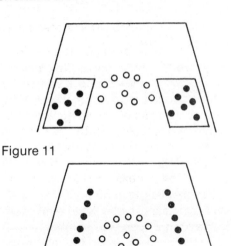

Figure 11

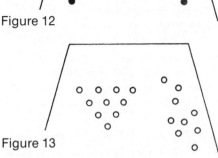

Figure 12

Figure 13

group on stage are positioned either much closer to each other or else much further apart than the singers in the raised chorus. Alternatively, a pleasing sense of asymmetry can be achieved if the singers are placed on one side of the stage during the danced numbers, as illustrated in Figure 13. The motionless singing chorus may even provide the dancers with a human climbing frame, or a human maze to run through or hide behind. In Figure 14 the motionless chorus kneel whilst the two lovers partake in a game of chase, as would be appropriate to use in a song such as 'Come One' (Beowulf). Singers do not necessarily need to watch events when the songs they sing refer to the ongoing action.

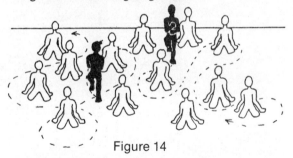

Figure 14

Movement for the Singing Chorus during a Small Group Dance

If it seems more appropriate for the singing chorus to move slightly during a dance, try using a continuously repeated movement, for example a constant steady swaying; a change of weight from one foot to another; a bending of the knees; a rising onto the balls of the feet and then lowering. The presence of movement such as this is often more appropriate for the rhythmic or fast tempoed number than complete stillness. Stillness may well be misinterpreted as a kind of perverse stubborness or may lead to a blocked, tense feel about the musical. If more energy is needed than swaying or the equivalent can supply, try marching on the spot or clapping. In Figure 15 the chorus group is gesturing quite energetically during the danced quartet but with repeated and simple movement so as not to act as a distraction. The chorus members repeatedly lift off

Figure 16

their hats to the side, using three beats to perform the lift and one beat to return it to their heads. After doing this eight times, they change hands and perform the same action on the other side. In Figure 16 the chorus will simply bend and stretch their arms repeatedly in the open symmetrical position. Too many changes of activity are liable to take attention away from the dancers. An extremely simple change of activity on the other hand, will not be distracting. An example of this would be if the singers

performed 8 beats of swaying, followed by 8 beats of marching, followed by 8 beats of clapping. Or if a simple sequence of changing symmetrical arm gestures was used as demonstrated in Figure 17.

Figure 17

Movement Interplay between Chorus and Dancing Group

An interplay of singing chorus and soloist dancers is often highly exciting. It is possible to decide on an order of events before setting the choreography, for example, soloists, then chorus, then both together, then chorus, then both, then soloists, then both.

The singing chorus may on occasions join in with the simple symmetrical movements of the dancing group. It would not of course be sensible for the singing chorus to 'join in' with the more complex and energetic stepping patterns due to space limitations, masking problems and breathlessness. The chorus may also at times perform contrasting movements to those of the soloists, turn when the soloists jump for example, or jump when the soloists turn. Use contrasts discriminately, however. If the couple are dancing with a long succession of flowing arm gestures for example, there would be too much confusion if the chorus danced with different arm patterns. It may be better for them in these circumstances simply to put their hands by their sides.

Figure 15

3. General Vocabulary

'Select image - provoking movement'
(L. Ellfeldt, *A Primer for Choreographers*, p36)

This section does not pretend to be a comprehensive guide to movement vocabulary, but provides tips concerning ways of finding and using steps and body designs. It may be reasuring to know, however, that when choreographing musicals, a visual common sense concerning body and spatial design is often more important than having a wide vocabulary of complex steps and a strong technical ability. In other words, when choreographing musicals it is often more useful to learn to *see* rather than to learn to *move*.

If the choreographer has absolutely no dance experience, there are usually one or two people in the cast with some tap or ballet experience who can set some of the stepping problems for the solo, duo or trio dance.

Capturing a Style

A musical often incorporates a whole range of different dance styles, for example, social dance, tap, ballet, jazz, ballroom, waltzing, tango, folk dance, and dance from different countries. If, however, dances in a set style are incorporated into the choreography they are often adapted or changed slightly to suit the musical's particular idiom. In many ways the musical has closed the gap between social and theatre dance and increasingly so with the rise of the modern rock musical, the choreography of which is often founded on a complex interrelationship of a tremendous variety of styles. The choreography in *Saturday Night Fever*, for example, is a mix of ballroom dancing, Spanish dance, jazz, disco and acrobatics. Jazz dance itself, sometimes thought of as the mother of vocabulary for musical choreography, is a mixed style, with its parallel placing, low stance and syncopated rhythms of African origin and its elegant refinement due to a later merger with English social dance. American tap dancing, closely related to jazz, originally grew out of English clog dancing.

With choreography for musicals, authenticity or purity of the style is often of less importance than whether the style has rhythm, pace and energy. Sometimes it is sufficient simply to capture the essence or flavour of a style. Completely accurate renderings are not usually essential. The following books and videos may be useful references for learning a particular style of dance. When watching a video, remember that a 'style' is like a dye running through every element of the choreography, but is particularly noticeable in use of rhythm, carriage of the torso, use of feet, presence or absence of isolations, amount of space used and tempo. Therefore analyse videos from those viewpoints in particular.

Films, Video Tapes and Books Suitable for Quick Research

1. Ballet

Video Tapes/Films - MUSICALS
An American in Paris - 16 mm Film (Harris Films Ltd)
Hair - VHS/Beetamax Video Tape (Intervision Video Ltd)
Oklahoma - VHS/Beetamax Video Tape (MGM/CBS Records)

Video Tapes/Films - GENERAL
Ballerina - 16 mm Film (Scottish Central Film Library)

Curtain Up - 16 mm Film (Guild Sound and Vision Ltd)
Harmony - 16 mm Film (Scottish Central Film Library)
Pas de Deux - 16 mm Film (Harris Films Ltd)
Books
The Kay Ambrose Ballet Companion edited by J. Lawson, (A. & C. Black, London, 1979)
The Art of Pas de Deux by J. Lawson, & N. Serrebrenikov, (Dance Books Ltd, London 1978)

2. Country Dance/Folk Dance
Video Tapes/Films - MUSICALS
Oklahoma - VHS/Beetamax Video Tape (MGM/CBS, CBS Records)
Seven Brides for Seven Brothers - 16 mm Film (Harris Films Ltd)
Video Tapes/Films - GENERAL
Billingham International Folklore Festival - 16 mm Film (Scottish Central Film Library)
Cumberland Square Dance - 16 mm Film (National Audio Visual Aids Library)
The Rose Tree (Morris Dance) - 16 mm Film (National Audio Visual Aids Library)
Books
Country Dance Steps by T. Leisner, (Chartwell Books Inc., New Jersey, 1980)
Your Book of English Country Dancing by P. & P. Lobley, (Faber & Faber, London, 1980)
Let's Dance Country Style by R. Smedley & J. Tether (Granada Publishing, London, 1982)

3. Disco Dance/Jazz Dance
Video Tapes/Films - MUSICALS
All That Jazz - VHS/Beetamax Video Tape (CBS/Fox Video)
Fame - VHS/Beetamax Video Tape (MGM/CBS, CBS Records)
Grease - VHS/Beetamax Video Tape (CIC Video UIP House)
Saturday Night Fever - 16 mm Film (Rank Film Library)
West Side Story - VHS/Beetamax Video Tape (Intervision Video Ltd)
Video Tapes/Films - GENERAL
British Hustle - 16 mm Film (Rank Film Library)
Music Machine - 16 mm Film (Harris Films Ltd)
Books
Jazz Dancing. An Adult Beginners Guide by H. Andreu (Prentice Hall Inc., New Jersey, 1983)
The Official Guide to Dancing by A. Dow (Chartwell Books Inc., New Jersey, 1983)
The Matt Mattox Book of Jazz Dance by E. Frich (Sterling Publishing Co. Inc., New York, 1983)

4. Tap Dancing
Video Tapes/Films - MUSICALS
All That Jazz - VHS/Betamax Video Tape (CBS/Fox Video)
Carefree - 16 mm Film (Harris Films Ltd)
The Gay Divorcee - 16 mm Film (Harris Films Ltd)
42nd Street - 16 mm Film (Harris Films Ltd)
Top Hat - VHS/Betamax Video Tape (Dance Books Ltd)

Video Tapes/Films - GENERAL
Tap Dancin' - 16 mm Film (Concord Arts Council of Great Britain)

Books
The Robert Audy Method of Tap Dancing by R. Audy (Random House Inc., New York, 1976)
The Basic Technique of Tap by M. Gay (ISTD, London, 1979)
Tap Dancing Step by Step by T. Sinibaldi (Sterling Publishing Co. Inc., New York, 1982)
Basic Tap Dancing by D. Washbourne (Russell Turner, London, 1979)

5. Ballroom and Latin American Dance

Note: Ballroom dancing is particularly pleasing if it is combined with more abstract dance. After a while, for example, the dancers may move out of their ballroom holds and face the front of the stage in order to perform unison movements separately, and then return to their ballroom holds. Alternatively, try interspersing ballroom dancing with lifts and supports. The 'freeze' of a waltzing couple 'mid-step' is often very visually attractive.

Video Tapes/Films - MUSICALS
The King and I - VHS/Betamax Video Tape (CBS/Fox Video)
My Fair Lady - VHS/Betamax Video Tape (MGM/CBS, CBS Records)

Vidoe Tapes/Films - GENERAL
The Story of Vernon and Irene Castle - 16 mm Film (Harris Films Ltd)

Books

The Revised Technique of Latin American Dancing (Imperial Society of Teachers of Dancing, London, 1983)
Teach Yourself Ballroom Dancing by The Imperial Society of Teachers of Dancing (Hodder & Stoughton, London, 1983)
Latin and American Dances by D. Lavelle (A. & C. Black, London, 1983)
Ballroom Dancing by A. Moore (A. & C. Black, London, 1983)
How to Dance by D. Muir (Omnibus Press, London, 1977)
Better Dancing by L. B. Wainwright (Kaye & Ward Ltd, Surrey, 1983)

6. Quick Reference

For quick reference for a number of styles, e.g. tap, ballroom, jazz, see:

That's Entertainment I, *That's Entertainment* II - VHS/Betamax Video Cassette (MGM/CBS, CBS Records)

and most Fred Astaire/Gene Kelly musicals. The following musicals are all 16 mm films - Distributor: Harris Films Ltd:

A Damsel in Distress, The Band Wagon, Blue Skies, Easter Parade, Shall We Dance, Silk Stockings, Invitation to the Dance, On the Town and Singing in the Rain

Addresses of Film Distributors

Guild of Sound and Vision Ltd 6 Royce Road, Peterborough PE1 5YB. Tel. 0733 315315
Harris Films Ltd/Glenbuck Films Glenbuck Road, Surbiton, Surrey KT6 6BT. Tel. 01 399 0022
National Audio Visual Aids Library Paxton Place, Gipsy Road, London SE27 9SR.
Rank Film Library PO Box 20, Great West Road, Brentford, Middlesex TW8 9HR.
Scottish Central Film Library 16/17 Woodside Terr. Charing Cross, Glasgow C3. Tel. 041 334 9314
Video and Films Council (Arts Council) 201 Felixstowe Road, Ipswich, Suffolk. Tel. 0473 726012

Addresses of Video Cassette Distributors

CBS/Fox Video Unit 1, Perivale Industrial Park, Greenford, Middlesex. Tel. 01 997 2552
CIC Video UIP House, 45 Beadon Road, Hammersmith, London W6 0EG. Te. 01 741 9041
Dance Books Ltd 9 Cecil Court, London WC2N 4EZ. Tel 01 836 2314
Intervision Video Ltd
          Unit 10, Osiers Estate, Enterprise Way, Wandsworth, London SW18. Tel. 01 870 0159
MGM/CBS, CBS Records Distribution Centre, Barlby Road, London W10. Tel. 01 969 3277

Certain Basic Guidelines in Choosing Vocabulary

There are certain basic guidelines which should be followed when choreographing movement vocabulary. These are outlined below:

Avoid Clichéd Vocabulary

For example, Tiller girl leg kicks, or slowly raising the arms to position at the end of number. Try to surprise the spectator with the 'unexpected', the movement firework.

Avoid Anachronism

Don't, for example, include charleston steps in a musical set in the late 1800s, simply because a member of your cast can perform a charleston very well. Be aware of all out-of-style movements which often bring with them a whole host of unhelpful associations.

Avoid Over-repetition of Certain Gestures

The choreographer may reach the end of his work only to find that he has used position

in five numbers and position

in seven dances, in four of which he used this design as the end position! Scan work for repetitions in the early stages of rehearsing.

Do Not Use Movements Inappropriate to the Size of the Stage

On a full stage it is possible to convey a feeling of movement energy without very much energy being expended, and very little whole body movement being performed. If a large chorus uses peripheral gestures and travels any distance sideways, backwards or forwards, this will tend to expose how little space there is.

Avoid Choreographing Movements which the Spectator Will Not be Able to See

For example, complex stepping patterns in a chorus group of 16 people who are dancing all on the same level, will be largely masked or unseen.

Do Not Work From the Assumption that there is a One to One Relationship Between a Movement and its Meaning

Some steps and movements have certain associations or connections. An upright symmetrical stance, for example, often conveys a sense of confidence and stability; a horizontal lying position with head resting on hand can indicate relaxation or calmness, a jump can suggest happiness. Remember, however, that dance is unlike verbal language. Each movement is very much dependent on its particular context for its meaning.

Avoid Illogical Transitions

If words are put together haphazardly in speech the result is often nonsense. It is equally important to make a comprehensible statement with movements and, therefore, to avoid illogical transitions and a disjointed succession of movements. When choreographing each new movement, bear in mind the probable preceding and following movement and its place in the overall structure of the dance.

Finding New Movements

Everyone has an extensive movement vocabulary. The problem is how to become aware of it and how to tap it. Everyday movements, for example are a delightful source of vocabulary. Using literal gesture and movement, the action of washing, ironing, walking, brushing teeth for example with a little exaggeration and rhythmic structuring to ensure it is dance not mime, can be delightful. Such gestures can also easily be transformed into more abstract movement by structured experimental exercises of trying out certain alterations in turn, e.g. by changing their shape in space; performing them with a different set of body parts;

trying them backwards or upside down; performing them larger or smaller, slower, faster, on a different level, in a different direction or with a different pathway; changing their dynamic qualities. If this process of distortion, abstraction, variation and change is used with even supposedly mundane mimes like digging the garden or putting on make-up in front of a mirror, so that they no longer suggest these original actions, it is possible to find a whole wealth of highly original movements. If choreographers do not use structured ways such as this to find new vocabulary (particularly in terms of gestures) and instead just stand in front of the mirror and improvise, it is likely that they will tend to merely reproduce one of their habitual movements or movement patterns. Structured exercises are often needed to break away from movements being confined to the same straightjacket. Having once managed to 'break out' it will soon become apparent that there is a readily available vocabulary on tap whenever it is wanted.

Another way of finding movements is to spend the early rehearsal sessions with the dancers experimenting in enjoyable ways resemblant of children's games. This entails setting up a movement situation with rules; two examples to illustrate this are set out below:

(i) Teach a movement phrase then ask the dancers to perform it only under certain circumstances. They might, for example, be asked simply to skip around the room wherever they like but if they pass left shoulders with someone they are to stop and perform the taught movement phrase before continuing skipping again.

(ii) Ask each dancer to start to count to 10 silently at whatever speed he likes, then to fall or run up to someone before starting to jog around the room where he likes. In addition he should vibrate with his left arm within two feet of the wall, should rub someone's back if he has passed them three times, and all dancers should run to the back wall and huddle together if they see someone sitting on the floor.

In many ways all this may sound crazy, but such 'rule orientated' movement activities are excellent ways of finding spatial relationships, floor patterns and sequences of events and interactions that the imagination would never have dreamed up. Having watched the 'game', which has been set up in progress, the choreographer may then choose to discard most of what he sees, but he will often find something worth keeping and building on as part of his choreography.

Dance can evolve out of, or be a natural development from, physical activity. It is possible, for example, to draw much choreographic inspiration (as opposed to set steps) from such fields of human movement as sports; ritual events such as certain kinds of processions; ritual gestures like waving, shaking hands, and other forms of dance - social dance, folk dance. Ideas for all these can be distorted, abstracted, changed, varied as suggested previously. Take, for example the idea of going underneath the arches which is used in folk dance. In Figure 1 this same idea is

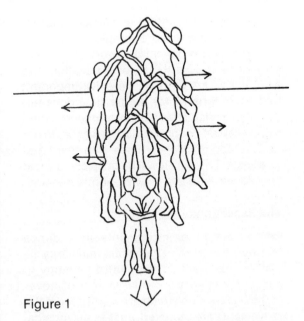

Figure 1

being used for a happy, jazzy number such as 'America' (*West Side Story*) but here the actual arches move, three steps to the right, five to the left, as the people walk through and cross. In Figure 2 the peeling off idea used in country

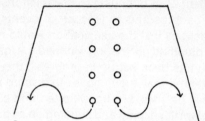

Figure 2

dance is shown, and could be a lovely way to change formation in a musical. Similarly, the familiar two rows (long ways set) moving in and out and crossing can be adapted and perhaps replicated or used with various directions (see Figure 3). The folk dance 'chain' is a very

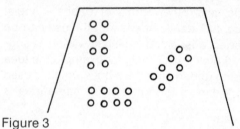

Figure 3

useful formation pattern in musical choreography if used with more complex vocabulary than in a country dance. One word of warning. The element of disguise or adaptation and alteration is very vital with these. It is important that choreography for the musical does not look like a plagiarised country dance! When using adapted country dance formation do not use the country dance steps with them and vice versa. This way it will be possible to avoid 'too close' associations with country dancing.

The Repetition of Movements

The repetition of movements in a dance number, the pleasure of their familiarity, is just as important as the use of leitmotiv in music. The spectator carries images of movements in his mind which are reinforced if the movements are repeated. Just as the musical has recurring tunes in overture, preformance and reprise of the music, similarly choreography benefits from occasionally repeating a movement sequence. Repetition can be

used as a device to re-emphasise something important in terms of the spectator's understanding of a theme or event or particular moment in time.

An image can be slightly changed, varied or camouflaged when repeated. Beware of over-disguising however. Many repeats will often remain unacknowledged by the spectator, unless they are very obvious and clear. The mind will not retain information about a muddle or some over-complex sequence. Be selective, pick the really eye catching movements to repeat. Furthermore it is often the case that, due to its comparative familiarity, illustrative or literal gesture needs less repetition for an image to be remembered than abstract gesture. Also be careful not to leave too long a time lapse before repeating a movement. Memories of images soon fade. Conversely, however, do not repeat too much. An obvious example of this can be seen in the common misuse of canon. In a group of 12 dancers, for example, when number eight dancer has performed a movement in exactly the same way as the previous seven numbers, one assumes that the four remaining numbers will also dance the same movement when it comes to their turn. Sadly one is usually right! Too often choreography includes redundant repeats as if a choreographer is attempting to force an image into the spectator's memory - most unpleasant!

Where and When to Repeat

Both over-repeating and badly placed repeats can be easily misinterpreted as the choreographer's paucity of vocabulary, provoking a response of 'not that again'. (Incidentally, this is often one of the biggest worries the novice choreographer has about repetition, which is why he often avoids it or uses it too rarely.) It is important, therefore to consider the full range of ways of repetition.

Various Ways and Times to Repeat:

1. At the time* (see below)
2. Later in the same dance
3. Later in the musical but in another dance

4. The repetition of a whole sequence, e.g. ABA, or rondo form
5. Repetition but with variation and/or development.

At the Time

This means performing two or more of the same movements in a dance one after another before moving on to performing a different movement (e.g. three identical spins, or a series of bobbing up and down movements). A dance without any repetition of a movement immediately succeeding its first performance can feel like too much to take in for the spectator. Note how tired the eye gets 'reading' Figure 4 which is little more than a disjointed

ℵ ||| △▽ ⌐ □ \\\ ∘∘ ○ ≡ ||| ✳ △ ○ □

Figure 4

string of disconnected symbols and how much easier it is to register Figure 5, and how much more pleasing it is as a result. It is always possible to slow down a movement to ensure that the spectator notices it or takes it in, but sometimes performing it more than once at the time is a far more effective device.

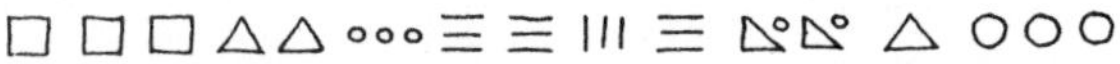

□ □□ △△ ∘∘∘ ≡ ≡ ||| ≡ ℵℵ △ ○○○

Figure 5

Body Parts and the Effect of the Isolation

The body is analogous to a full orchestra. The 'parts' can be played all together at times and separately at others. The feet, for example, may adopt a different dynamic quality, use of space and accenting than the upper body or head in the forming of one particular body design or movement. It is important not to play the 'full orchestra' all of the time, otherwise the specific beauty of some 'instruments' may not be fully appreciated. In other words, avoid a succession of whole body movements. Exploit the pleasure and subtlety which can be gained from the isolation, that is the use of one body part on its own or even a quick succession of different body parts. Then perhaps after a while return to the 'full orchestra'. Although many isolations are very small movements, if performed when the rest of the body is still,

they quickly attract attention. This section aims to highlight movement possibilities of certain body parts when used in isolation.

Hands

In every day non-verbal communication, hands are very expressive of emotional tensions and feelings. Isolated hand movements are, therefore, particularly useful to portray certain personality traits or idiosyncrasies in detailed choreographic characterisation; the nose picking finger gestures of punks for example or an evil character's spiky hands, or the 'tea drinking finger' of the snooty housewife. There is a whole wealth of possible hand positions to choose from. Fingers can be outstretched, together or curled into a fist. The palm can be facing the audience or the ceiling, or turned inwards towards the body. Wrists can be flexed or relaxed so that the hands are floppy. The thumb can be held away from the other fingers or next to them. The hand can point, wave, hang, quiver, ripple, curl or flicker. Alternatively the hands can be tidied away behind the back, under the braces, tucked into the belt or the arms folded. It is also possible to vary effects as illustrated in Figure 6 where

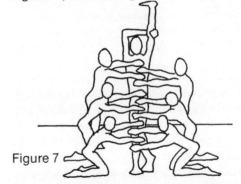

Figure 6

one hand is doing one thing whilst the other does another. Hands can be used as a way of disguise or concealment. They can also be placed over the face, for example, or a group can form a wall with their hands in front of them which masks most of their bodies from the spectator's view, or a wall of hands can be used to cover one dancer (see Figure 7) a choreographer could use in a

Figure 7

number such as 'Let Me Entertain You' (*Gypsy*).

Hand isolations are usually very noticeable in a close group, in the static singing chorus, for example, where apart from the hands, the body is still.

Feet

Feet are an integral and important part of any choreographic stance. They should be given 'choreographic' attention, even if a performer is going to be still throughout a song. Again there is a huge range of possible movements with the feet to choose from. Think of all the different parts of the foot: sole; ball; heel; instep; toe. Consider the flexed foot, feet together or apart, in parallel, turned out (heels together) or crossed (see Figure 8).

Figure 8

Experiment with different contacts with the ground: stamp; tap; brush; rub; glide; dab; massage; tiptoe, moving with the heels off the ground. Then try out different ways of stepping or transferring weight from one foot to another: stepping with a frequent change of direction; skipping; leaping; bouncing; slinking; striding; running; swaying; marching. Do not forget to consider size of step. Some foot positions can add decoration and detail to an otherwise plain movement. In Figure 9, for example, the one flexed foot adds an interesting variation to this leg gesturing jump.

Figure 9

Naturally though, complex patterns and foot play are better suited to solos and duos and some linear formed groups than to the larger groups where most of the feet are hidden or masked from view.

It is possible to compose easy and effective movement sequences by combining a few steps using a clear rhythmical structure - gallops, skips, sways and simple rises on the balls of the feet are not to be underestimated in choreography for musicals.

Simple Stepping Ideas and Combinations
l refers to the left, r to the right

Little runs on the spot or little runs travelling; effective when used in a curving floor pattern or procession, for example as demonstrated in Figure 10.

Step together step touch.

Sway sway step together step.

Step hop jump stamp then ¼ turn.

Step touch step touch step together step touch (touch refers to a light tap with the ball of the foot).

Step touch step touch stamp stamp stamp.

Side step and bend, step touch bend (repeat to the other side)

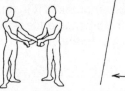

Figure 10
Little jumping steps from one to the other

Stamp (r) toe heel (l) stamp (r) toe heel (r) (toe heel is a light rap on the floor with the gesturing foot then the heel)

'The square' - start crossing right leg over left, step diagonally back on the left to left corner
then: diagonally back on the right to right corner
then: through straight forward as on the left leg

Sway sway step turn sway

Marching on the spot

On the spot step click (low to the right side) step click (low to the left side)

Step click (high to the right side) step click (high to the left side) (the clicking is done with both hands)

Cat steps (high to knee crossing steps) (see Figure 11)

Figure 11

Step right, step left, step together step (repeat other way)

Step turn step together step

Step back feet together step forward kick
(r)   (l joining the r)   (r)

Walking a figure of eight

Walk forward right left right kick (l) ball change kick (l) touch (l) to the side then touch together (l)

Walking with exaggerated steps with pronounced elbows, or high straight arms and stretched legs not bent at the knees

The *pas de bourée* - step behind with the right leg to the side with the left and cross in front with the right

Four runs on the spot, four turning (take the knees higher than in normal jogging).

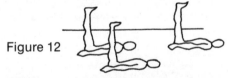

Figure 12

Legs

A gesturing leg can add an element of decoration to an otherwise symmetric design. When using leg kicks it is possible to avoid unhelpful connotations with Tiller girls by decorating the kick slightly with an isolation, perhaps of the shoulder or head. If there are bodies on the floor, legs coming up to make a right angle with the torso can be very effective as illustrated in Figure 12 and Figure 13.

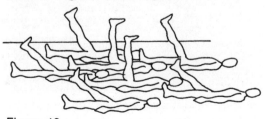

Figure 13.

Knees and Hips

Starting a dance with bent-kneed positions is often visually very pleasing and produces a very neat design for a whole crowd if used with no additional decoration to the position or other isolation. It can also suggest an anticipation of action. Gangsters, as for example, in the number 'Luck Be a Lady Tonight' (*Guys and Dolls*) may bend and stretch their knees whilst aggressively clicking their fingers, torso bending forwards, as the opening part of a dance. It can be effective to echo bent knees with arms bent to the same angle. Also the bent-kneed 'second position' (ballet terminology) can be visually very impactive when used for a large group as shown in Figures 14 and 15 a & b. This is due mainly to the beauty and clarity of the right angle. The second position

Figure 14   Figure 15a

Figure 15b

can be travelled jumped or turned. A possible combination of these suggestions would be three second position jumps on the spot followed by a second position half-turn to face the back and then a half turn to face the front again. Also try knock-kneed positions and all manner of crouching and kneeling positions (see Figure 16).

Figure 16
Hips

Just as the 'knee wobble' should not be underestimated in choreography for musicals, so too can the hip wiggle add a degree of delightful decoration to an over simple position, particularly if the hips are used in isolation. Hips can also be effective when moved in the opposite direction to the rest of the body as illustrated in Figure 17.

Figure 17

Torso Tilts and Leans

The tilted torso produces a very clear line, and is particularly attractive when used facing the side as shown in Figure 18 a, b, c and d. In

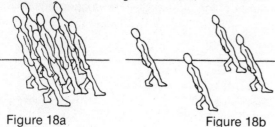

Figure 18a   Figure 18b

Figure 18c

Figure 18d

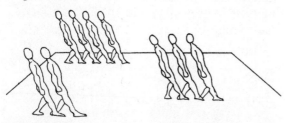

Figure 19 two torsos are tilting together as the couple face each other. One leans forward, the other back. They walk like this, keeping in close proximity and then exchange leaning positions to walk in the opposite direction. Or try a syncopated crossing movement of one

Figure 19

torso over another, with performers using eye contact in the tilt (see Figure 20). A large group may perform a succession of torso movements back and forth and side to side with a syncopated rhythm.

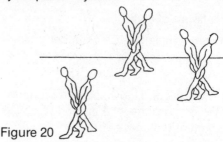

Figure 20

The success of the torso tilt depends on each member of the group having exactly the same torso angle and ensuring that the arms are held firmly to the sides of the body so as not to detract from the simplicity and clarity of the design. Figure 21 demonstrates a sitting down variation of the torso tilt and Figure 22

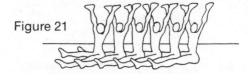

Figure 21

depicts 'the moving block'. Here the rows of people on different levels all place their hands on shoulders in front of them and use torso leans to peer forwards. It may on occasions, be

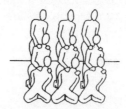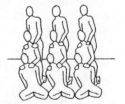

Figure 22

appropriate to introduce a slight decoration to the torso by the addition of another limb or limbs, as for example the arms design shown in Figure 23a and b.

Figure 23a

Figure 23b

Other Torso Effects

Sometimes the torso can lean or move into a different direction to that of the lower body or head. In Figure 24, for example, the torso is

Figure 24

facing the front of the stage but the head and lower body and feet are facing the side. The torso is often highly expressive of certain emotional states. The stoop in Figure 25a for

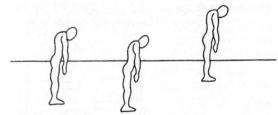

Figure 25a

example, would be ideal for a downtrodden group such as the group of children who sing

'We'd Like to Thank You Herbert Hoover' from the musical *Annie*. Figure 25b illustrates a

Figure 25b

much more extreme version of this. Try a sudden change from a long sequence of arm gestures in a dance to using no arms and just torso movements. Figure 26 illustrates one possible

Figure 26

transition for an arm gestured movement to a torso lean. A succession of different torso leans, as would be appropriate in a number like 'A Policeman's Lot is Not a Happy One' (*Pirates of Penzance*) can be particularly pleasing as illustrated in Figure 27.

Figure 27

Flat Back

A flat back position can be effective due to the right angle which is formed with the body (see Figure 28a and b). Figure 29 depicts a slightly more decorated version of a flat back design.

Figure 28a and b

Figure 29

Shoulders

The shoulders can move up and down, forward and back, together or one at a time (see Figure 30). A syncopated combination of varying directional shoulder movements whilst the rest of the body is completely still, is often delightful. Shoulder isolations by their very nature are so small that they can sometimes be missed in the distant group. They tend to be more effective, therefore, when performed in a close group.

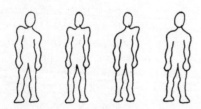

Figure 30

Heads

Head isolations are arguably the most effective isolations of all. Heads moving in unison back and forth from point A to point B can produce a stunning hypnotic effect. This can gain additional interest with the use of a syncopated rhythm. For example:

Beats		
1 &		heads move to the left
2		heads move to the right
3 & 4 &		heads move to the left
5		heads move to the right
&		heads move to the left
6		heads move to the right
		(Hold for 7 8 9)
& 10		heads move to the left

The change from heads being used as part of a whole body movement to suddenly being used in isolation, whilst the rest of the body remains motionless, can be stunning. To ensure that a head isolation is particularly noticeable, keep the rest of the body facing in a different direction from that of the head (see Figure 31). The

(Figure 31)

head movement in an otherwise 'plain walk' is effective, just as are other 'isolation' walks such as the 'hip-wiggle-walk', and the 'torso-lean-walk'. Or heads can be 'isolated' in the sense that the rest of the body is hidden. Heads can appear over a wall, for example, as they do in Figure 32.

Figure 32

Arms, Symmetry and Order

Arms play a major role in choreography for musicals, perhaps more so than any other body parts. This is particularly true for chorus group work. The most suitable arm designs for a chorus group are often those using symmetry. That is where both arms are doing exactly the same. Figure 33 shows three possible

Figure 33

sequences of symmetrical arm positions, using the appealing opening and closing, raising and lowering ideas. These simple symmetrical movements are always very attractive but beware of over-use and clichés such as the slow raising of the arms into a high V. Another effective use of the arms is the dissolving of symmetry. In Figure 34 for example, the body slowly melts into a state of asymmetry. As previously mentioned, arms symmetrically placed in front of the body can be used as 'space-saving-devices' (see Figure 35)

Figure 34

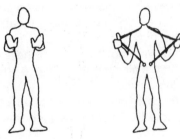

Figure 35

A symmetrical use of the arms ensures tidiness and can prevent blocking problems. Figure 36 shows what can happen to a beautiful asymmetrical arm pattern if adopted by a close group. It looks here rather like a child's scribble, one line interfering or merging with the

Figure 36

next, whereas in Figure 37 the symmetrical design remains both separate and clear when used in a close group. Symmetry can provide a close group with a sense of unity, togetherness and order. The stage can often accommodate a larger number of bodies if they adopt

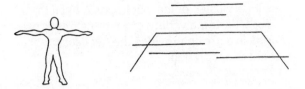

Figure 37

symmetrical as opposed to asymmetrical arm designs. Figure 38 illustrates how three separate groups happily co-exist even if the symmetrical movements are different and varied. Indeed groups having different symmetrical designs often complement each other. Conversely with the performance of asymmetrical designs, often the asymmetry of one group does not happily co-exist with that of another.

Symmetry is particularly pleasing and appropriate for a finishing position, it can provide a feeling of completeness and assurity. One word of warning. If both arms have been held high in the air for a long time, a sudden drop can feel to the audience as if the following movements have been stripped of some of their novelty. They can seem rather bare.

Figures 39

Figure 38

Figure 40

Asymmetry

Despite the problems mentioned above, asymmetry is sometimes useful to add a little more detail to an otherwise plain design, or to add a sense of tension or restlessness to a movement. Asymmetrical arm designs are particularly apt for the naturalistic group, the 'conversational cluster' or the 'photo pose'. In all these cases, having a variety of asymmetrical positions in a group provides the neccessary element of decoration.

41a

Angles

There are some asymmetrical arm positions which have the same ordering capacities and spatial clarity as symmetrical positions. For example in Figure 39 the asymmetry acts as broken summetry. Some asymmetrical and angular uses of arms are extremely clear - the right angle in particular as demonstrated in Figures 40 and 41 a & b.

41b

Curves and 'Tree-Wafting'

Some asymmetrical movements can deteriorate into undisciplined and vague wafting and a loss of sharp outline. Obviously the musical can afford none of these. An arm design must never be vague or ill-defined otherwise what is often a cluttered stage anyway in a musical, may become a chaotic state of untidyness. The curved arm pattern, particularly if coupled with free flowing movement, is particularly prone to such problems of lack of clarity. Notice, for example, the ambiguity with this movement. Is it an over straight curve or a weak right angle? Even if the curve does not 'waft about' but remains still, it is still usually extremely difficult to polish in a large group. Figure 42 illustrates a common problem where members of the group are all attempting to perform the same curved movement, but in each case the result is slightly

Figure 42

different. Curves, therefore are often best used with symmetry as shown in Figure 43a and b and Figure 44.

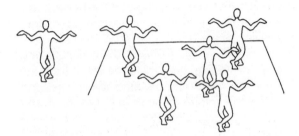

Figure 43a

Figure 43b

Figure 44

Examples of Effective Asymmetrical Designs

Below is a collection of asymmetrical designs which *are* both suitable for a large group and easy to perfect:

Figure 45. One arm designs. The other arm can be tidied away as part of the torso.

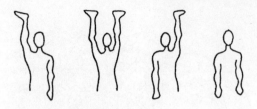

Figure 46. Changes from asymmetry to symmetry and vice-versa.

Figure 47. One arm is added to the design, thus the asymmetrical position becomes symmetrical for a while.

Figure 48 and Figure 49. Change from asymmetry on one side of the body to the other side.

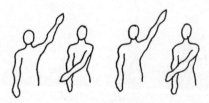

Figure 50. Diagonal reaching movements with one arm.

Mixed Isolations Within or Across Groups

These can be very visually appealing. In Figure 51 for example each group uses a different body part in isolation. Also isolations with different body parts used in quick succession can be exciting to watch.

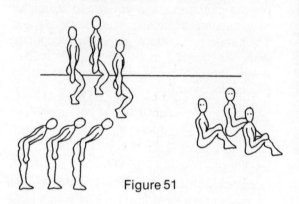

Figure 51

Activities

Turns

Turns can generate a great deal of energy, particularly if performed with speed. Carefully consider what sort of turn is likely to be appropriate for each dance or movement phrase, for example, an open, closed, high, low, travelled or jumped turn. Above all, keep turns tidy. Throwing the arms in any fashion can look very messy. When performers are unfamiliar with turning techniques, ask them to keep the arms tightly in as they turn. Multiple turns and those which require spotting should be avoided with untrained dancers. Use quarter or half turns instead. Poorly executed turns seem to highlight a performer's lack of dance training more than any other activity.

Dancers can often prevent themselves falling over or losing their balance in a turn, by lowering the body, bending the knees, and using the minimum amount of tension and energy to get round. Easy turns are outlined below:

1. Step together (½ turn to the right)
   Step together (another ½ to the right)
   Step step step step (full turn to the right)
   (see Figure 52 for use of arms)

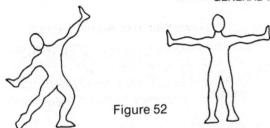

Figure 52

2. Fast turn on one leg - picking up the left leg, turn to the right on the right leg. Prevent falling or wobbling by putting the left leg down on the ground like a brake in a car after having turned.

3. Turn to the right by crossing the left foot well over the right (weight on right leg) then turn. In other words: a) knot up, b) turn, c) undo the knot.

4. Four quarter turning jumps, one to each direction - front side back side
    (l)   (r)

5. Face the back of the stage, then do a half turn suddenly to face the audience.

6. Different groups on stage may each use different directional turns. For example group A may perform three half turns to the right whilst group B perform two full turns to the back and group C perform a quarter turn to the left followed by two half turns to the right.

7. A line could perform a sequence of turns. For example, in unison two steps to the right, one step to the back, two steps to the front, one to the left, two to the back, finishing with one to the right.

8. Figure 53 demonstrates the ripple effect where the As turn towards the Bs. This energy then motivates the Bs to move. The Bs then have the same effect on the Cs and the Ds likewise. It is important for the canon to take over very quickly to produce a ripple.

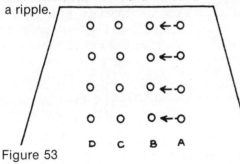

Figure 53

9. Crossing turns in a group. Two rows cross behind and two rows in front. The sequence is four turns to cross and two stamps, then cross back. This can produce a pleasing multi-activity effect with the simultaneous crossing and turning.

10. Accelerating turns ending in a jump - a very effective way for increasing energy to a climactic point.

Spinning

The speed of spinning can be exhilerating for the spectator to watch. There is often, however, a tendency to under estimate the space needed for a spin. Pre-plan carefully and realistically. Spinning is particularly appealing if performed with a clear and simple design, a torso lean for example as demon- strated in Figure 54. Wearing full skirts in a spin can increase the sense of energy and

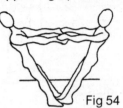

Fig 54

speed. Figure 55 shows slightly more decorated swivel turns. The two people are facing each other with hands round each other's waists and one arm out. They will need to lean out to

Figure 55

achieve the maximum possible speed. There is nothing worse than a spin that is 'too safe', in other words where performers are not prepared to trust each other and to lean out. A 'safe' spin often resembles a fairground roundabout with a cranky machine!

Special Spinning Effects

1. *The Basket.* The women put their hands round the men's necks and join hands with each other. The men hold the women round their waists and again join hands with each other. As they gather speed in the turn the women should let their legs fly into the air (see Figure 56). (This requires a lot of space!)

Figure 56

2. *The Star.* All four performers hold right arms in the middle, lean out, spin and then change direction. This is a simple idea, particularly useful momentarily or as part of a transition.

Jumps

Jumping is an excellent way of raising the energy level in a performance. Performed well and with speed, jumps can often lead to the spectator feeling exhilarated. Sometimes the simplest jumps, a two feet jump with no arm gesture, for example, are the most effective in a large group. Try dancers jumping over other dancers. Jumps fall under the following categories:

    Two feet to two feet
    One foot to two feet
    One foot to the other foot (leap)
    One foot to the same foot (hop)
    Two feet to one foot

Two feet to two feet jumps

1. *Pogo jumps.* Arms are held tightly in to the sides and feet kept together. Even if these jumps are not very high, they can be very energy producing, particularly if performed in a large spread out group. Try little pogo jumps on the spot in a close group but *not* in unison. This will look like heads bobbing up and down in the sea.

2. Figure 57
a) Hit knees with hands in the air (feet together)
b) Split jump (flexed hands and feet)
c) Jumps with legs in parallel or turned out
d) Arms circling in the air

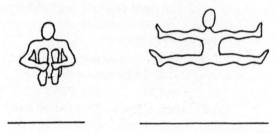

Figure 57a   Figure 57b

Figure 57c

Figure 57d

3. Changing direction '2—2' Jumps

In the following sequence the direction of the turns becomes delightfully unpredictable:

(i) Three to the front one to the right
(ii) Three to the front one to the left
(iii) One to the front, one to the right, one to the front, one to the left
(iv) Three to the front
(v) One full jumping turn all the way round

One foot to the other foot Jumps (Leaps)

1. Figure 58
   a) Step leap
   b) Stag leap

Figure 58a   Figure 58b

2. *Skips* on the spot or travelling
3. *Gallops* e.g. four to the right side, four to the left then two to the right, two to the left, then four skips on the spot.

One foot to the same foot Jumps (Hops)

1. Step hop with a bent supporting leg

2. Hop on the left leg tapping the right foot (four times)

Hop on the right leg tapping the left foot (four times)

Repeat two to the right leg, two to the left, then one to the right, one to the left, one to the right and one to the left.

3. *Heel-clicking Jump* - hit the upper leg on the underneath leg in the air (Figure 59). In other words, cross the left leg over the right, then click the heels to the right in the air, then cross the right leg over the left, and click the heels to the left in the air.

Figure 59

Other effects with Jumps

1. There are three rows of people as shown in Figure 60. The As (women) leapfrog over the Bs and dance in the arms of the men in row C. This would be appropriate for a hoe down (e.g. *Seven Brides for Seven Brothers*)

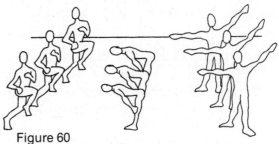

Figure 60

2. Jumps of monsters, goblins or space creatures can be performed with asymmetrical decorations, such as flicks, wriggles, spirals, or with isolated body parts, the shoulder, head, for example. The 'flight' of the grotesque jump can give added power to evil characters like those found in 'The Cyclopean Song' (*Ulysses*); 'Grendel's Song' (*Beowulf*); 'Dracula's Song' (*The Dracula Spectacular*); and in 'I'm Only Little' (*The Sweeny Todd Shock 'n' Roll Show*) (see Figure 61)

Figure 61

Falls

To avoid injury, ensure that the body is very relaxed and that the weight falls *downwards*, rather than forwards, backwards or out to the side somewhere. Aim to fall on 'fleshy bits', as opposed to elbows, knees or other joints. Ask performers to practise on a mat first. A group can run and fall in ripple canon as shown in Figure 62a. A startled reaction can be conveyed through a backwards fall in a line (see Figure 62b) or falling can be used in a more distant group who wish to hide or to react to fear. The sudden change of level resulting from such falling can be very pleasing, particularly with a slight embellishment of the heads in the hands where the performers arrive on the floor (see Figure 62c).

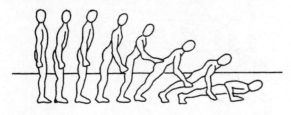

Figure 62a

Figure 62b

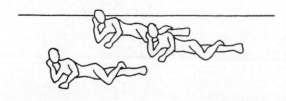

Figure 62c

Wiggling, Shaking, Vibrating, Shivering, Jiggling, Swaying and Pulsating

Any of these activities can be performed whilst travelling, jumping or turning. If all the people on a full stage shake or wiggle, the vibrating rhythm and resultant energy release is often electrifying. Such activities can be used to show feelings like fear, exasperation or hilarity. In Figure 63 the wiggling on the floor could be used to convey a whole range of emotional states. It would be particularly effective for example, in The Temple Scene in *Jesus Christ Superstar* to show the despair of the lepers and sightless people. Hand vibrating and body shaking can be very appealing when performed with backs to the audience.

Figure 63

Swaying

Individuals on stage can sway identically in unison or in different directions and with different rhythms and tempos. This is often mesmerising, although beware of a possible drawback of the audience feeling seasick if this is continued for too long! Swaying can be a simple changing of weight from one foot to the other with no upper body involvement. Alternatively, it can be a swaying of the upper body only or perhaps a successive movement from the shoulders to the lower body. It can be initiated in the ribs or hips or legs. Feet can be together or apart, in parallel or turned out during the swaying.

Energy Change

Wiggling, shaking, vibrating, shivering, jiggling or pulsating are all useful for radically or suddenly transforming the energy level of a dance from a calm and sustained use of energy for example to a sudden and fast state. Energy change is vital in choreography. The contrasting numbers in the musical, for example, ballad to patter song, build in their own energy change, but the choreographer should aim to build in more.

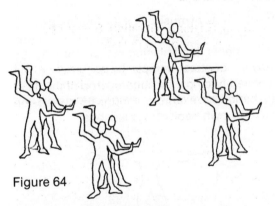

Figure 64

The Fascination of Duplication

Duplication is both noticeable and attractive. Identical twins, for example, are more eye-catching in a world of human individuality and lack of replica. Duplication can be used to emphasise the formality of an occasion or to produce humour. Think of the 'copycat', 'the mirror image', 'taking the mickey'. As previously stated, one can duplicate a movement whilst varying some elements, using a difference in level or direction for example.

Complementary Shapes

In Figure 64 identical body shapes are placed next to each other but one is lower than the other. These complementary shapes are particularly eye-catching if performed by more than one couple on stage at any one time. The slight difference in level between the person in front and the person behind helps to avoid masking, displays the two shapes more advantageously, and adds interest (see Figure 65a).

Figure 65a

Several couples on stage may alternatively all adopt a different duplication of complementary shapes (see Figure 65b).

Figure 65b

Juxtaposing and Overlapping

These are other ways of using duplication. Instead of one partner being lower than the other, the one stands a little to the side of the other, in other words, overlapping. It sometimes takes a while to find the right degree of overlap. Too much overlap can cause interference, masking, or even amputation! It can also easily be misread as poor spatial blocking. Figure 66 and Figure 67 demonstrate how repeated overlap is attractive.

Figure 66

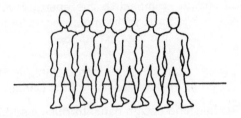

Figure 67

The Opening and Finishing Position

The Opening

The opening position in a choreography is important in that it is the first impression the spectator gets of a new and unfamiliar environment with a group of people unknown to him. It is sensible, therefore, to aim for easily and quickly identifiable opening designs, rather than random grouping, for example, which would be likely to make the spectator's initial adapting process quite difficult. A bombardment of stimuli of different movements and different forms of action may throw the spectator into a state of mild panic unless, of course, he is given sufficient time to take in this new environment. One way to ease the familiarisation process for the spectator is to start a dance number with a group freeze. Sometimes the poses in this may use literal illustrative gesture suggestive of the subject matter of the dance about to start. After the eye has had time to sufficiently scan the environment and its inhabitants, the characters may suddenly change into a moving group.

The Finish

Try and aim for a punchline, a heightening of interest and novelty at the very end. There is nothing worse than a dance which fizzles out with an anti-climax so that the spectator forgets the sparks and novelties which preceded it and leaves the show feeling depressed. Moreover, if the finish has little impact or energy, the dancers in the next number will have to work all the harder to generate enough energy to reach the optimum level again. Conversely, if the ending *is* impactive, the energy level is likely to rise through the applause and then be carried over into the next number.

Ways of introducing the Unpredictable and the Novel into the Last Moment of the Dance

The finishing design can introduce a sudden and unexpected change in level, direction or type of movement. A group could slowly rise to a high position, for example, immediately followed by an unexpected drop to the floor, or vice versa, a slow drop, and a sudden rise on the last note of music. Or if the final movement sequence has comprised mainly whole body movements, the finishing movement may, by way of contrast, simply be the use of one isolated body part, a sudden drop of the head or hand, for example. Figure 68 shows the head thrown back on the last beat.

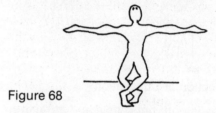

Figure 68

Interest can be gained from the sudden addition of physical contact in the finishing moments of a dance where previously the dancers have been separate. An example of this is the idea of the 'moving photo'. This is a finishing design where one member takes up a position. The second member then adopts a position relating closely to the first. The third member of the group then studies the duo and

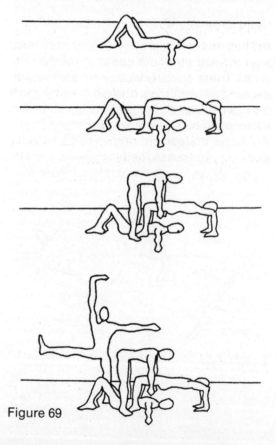

Figure 69

tries to adopt a pose which in some ways and to some extent fills the gaps which the two have created. Other members follow suit (see Figure 69). The group then attempts to move off stage in this position. This device could be used in a number such as 'Flash Bang Wallop' from the musical *Half a Sixpence*.

Lifts can provide an effective finish as can a sudden new patterning of the held props, taking hats off, or forming a wall or tower with hats for example. In Figure 70 the group who having been performing with their boards in unison throughout a dance, finish with each member in a different pose.

Figure 71

Figure 70

Above all, aim for a finish which is visually pleasing and which is sufficiently complex to be able to sustain interest during the applause, a finish using a variety of set and body levels, or a contrast of different groupings (see Figure 71). It is important to finish on the last note of music rather than before. Some numbers may end up with a fade out of the music, but this does not give license for the choreography to fizzle out. A sudden stop is far more impactive. Hold the freeze for a set number of beats during the fade down of music or lights.

Curtain Calls

Bows should be given a clear rhythmical phrase. The format of 'bow two-three, up two-three, grin two-three' sounds contrived but is effective. Performers should take their cue from the person in the most central downstage position. If the set has built-in levels, incorporate them into the group formation for the curtain calls. It is important to ensure that this part of the production is as visually pleasing as the rest of the choreography. Consider whether it is appropriate or not to bow in character.

4. Physical Contact

Consider the different degrees of physical contact and ways in which two or more dancers may share the same space from the slightest touch, to the simple support or lean, to the spectacular lift. Avoid using too much physical contact. Be sensitive to times in both fights and embraces when contact is better suggested rather than literally carried out, or where the words which the performers speak or sing are sufficient to establish a relationship. Two people standing closer than would be normal in terms of conversational distance can often say far more about the intensity of the affection they feel for each other than a passionate embrace. Do not avoid touching altogether however, otherwise some intended emotionally close relationships may appear unconvincing or odd. Physical contact can help to highlight important moments in a relationship. It can often convey more powerfully than words, protection, affection, comfort and anger. It can be used as the motivation to unleash energy into a dance, or it can be used purely for its design qualities. An effective transition can be to change from a group using much body contact to a unison group of individuals who dance a long way apart from each other.

Double Work

Supports

A support is a physical relationship where one or more dancers take part of the weight of another or other dancers. The supported person still keeps some contact with the ground whilst holding an off balance position. (This factor differentiates the support from the lift). If the dancer doing the supporting moved away, the person or people being supported would lose balance, wobble, or fall over according to the degree of support. Each support, therefore, necessitates an element of trust between participants. Supports can provide the excitement and 'risk value' of a lift without having so many of the potential problems of technique associated with lifting (e.g. dropping someone and not getting the correct grip).

A support can be a light hold of a small part of the body, a hand hold or a support on the back of the neck, or the whole body can be involved as in some lean or 'fall' supports. Any body parts can be in contact between 'supporter' and 'supported', a thigh can support a head, for example, or a forearm can support a leg.

Supports can also be more emotionally expressive than lifts. It is often difficult to maintain eye contact in a lift without ungainly neck craning on the part of both participants. Do not however over-estimate how long the spectator will want to look at a support or lift. Choreographers are often so pleased with the design created by supports or lifts that the positions are held too long and so lose both pace and tension. Performers must never stop and pose in a support but must move continually, however slowly it is. Think of supports, therefore, as part of an ongoing journey rather than as arrivals at a destination. One exception to this could be where a continuous sequence of supports has been built up and the final one may be held for a while, acting as a full stop. Never introduce the 'full stop' prematurely, however, before there has been a sufficient build up of energy. A flowing succession of supports is often delightful. The sequence below describes an exchange of energy between the 'supporter' and 'supported' and the dissolving of one support or touch into another.

Sequence of Supports and Touches for One Man and One Woman

Counts -

1 and 2	He touches her head
3	She touches his cheek
and 4	She leans on his shoulder and he pushes her gently
5 and 6	As she falls, he catches her back arm
6	and swings her round
and 7	She falls backwards and he supports her back with his hand.

This example also serves to illustrate how pleasing it can be, in terms of energy change, to juxtapose touch contacts (e.g. stroke, touch) with whole body supports. It can also be delightful to have couples or a couple performing a sequence of supports against a background of separate people.

Finding Supports

To find and create a whole realm of supports, the following starting points are possible:

1. One dancer forms a body design. The supporter then studies this shape in view of its potential places for support. He then tries out different contacts of various limbs and ways of taking some of his partner's weight so as to enable her to adopt an off balance position.

2. One dancer adopts a body design. Her partner then echoes the line of the design with his own body and takes some of his partner's weight in this position.

3. One partner stands behind the other. They stretch out their arms and hold hands (see Figure 1). They then experiment with taking each other's weight, by turning, to the side,

Figure 1

leaning, lowering, etc., whilst maintaining the hand hold. Alternatively, partners can experiment by standing side by side or face to face and hold both hands before them as before.

A Note about Technique

Supports are, by and large, technically more simple than lifts. With any support, however, it is essential that the supported person maintains body tension. A relaxed human body is always very difficult to support. Supports look unconvincing if dancers do not trust their partners sufficiently to allow them to take some of their weight.

It is always possible to tell if a dancer is only pretending to be 'off balance'.

Examples of Supports

1. Leans

(a) Front person leans on back person's chest (Figure 2a).

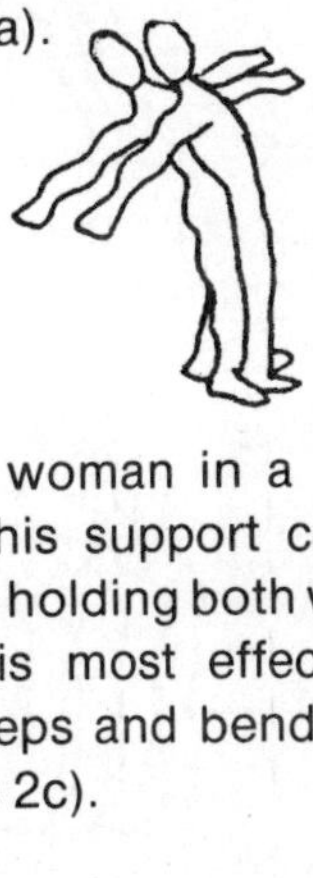

Figure 2a

(b) Man supports woman in a back bend (Figure 2b). This support can be performed by man holding both wrists of his partner. This is most effective if she tenses her biceps and bends her arms slightly (Figure 2c).

Figure 2b

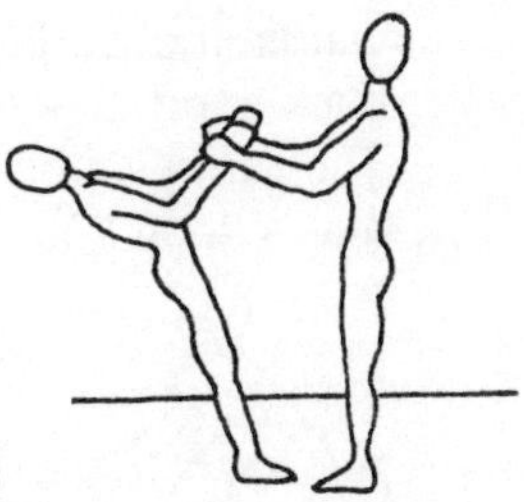

Figure 2c

(c) Woman is supported on man's back (see Figure 2d). With additional hand contact, the woman can be dragged off by hug-

Figure 2d

ging to the man's chest in this position, facing downwards as opposed to looking up at the ceiling.

(d) Woman leans on the side of man's body. He lunges to the side to support her weight (see Figure 2e).

Figure 2e

(e) A group of people all lean on each other (see Figure 2f).

Figure 2f

2.   Neck Holds

(a) Woman's torso and face are turned towards the audience in her supported back bend. She holds on to man's neck. The same support can be performed on man's knee (Figure 3a and b).

Figure 3a

Figure 3b

(b) Woman leans back keeping a very erect spine and man supports her with one hand on the back of her neck (see Figure 3c). He can also do this whilst kneeling down.

Figure 3c

(c) Woman stands facing man, hanging on to his neck with both hands. He then bends forwards and she slides through his legs, keeping her feet together whilst still maintaining contact with his neck.

3.   Pose Supports

Pose supports are contacts where the woman holds a position in which it is difficult for her to stay on balance without that additional support on the part of her partner:

(a) Woman leans towards man, her leg on his shoulder (see Figure 4a).

Figure 4a

(b) Man holds his arms out to the side and tenses them. Woman balances in a pose on one leg by holding onto one of her partner's outstretched arms with two hands (see Figure 4b)

Figure 4b

4. Mutual Supports

Mutual supports are supports when both partners rely on each other equally for physical support. Often this entails their pulling away from each other:

(a) The couple lean away from each other (Figure 5a).

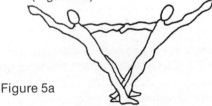

Figure 5a

(b) The couple pull away from each other in a flat back position (Figure 5b).

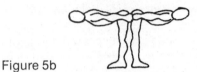

Figure 5b

(c) The couple face each other, lean out and by firmly pressing their 'inside' feet together, one of them can then lift a leg (Figure 5c).

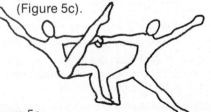

Figure 5c

Fall Supports

A fall support is a support when a dancer takes some of his partner's weight during a 'fall':

(a) Woman falls back on to man's thigh (see Figure 6a).

Figure 6a

(b) Woman falls back into man's arms. She keeps her feet on the floor. He turns her

round in this position. Half a turn to the back, then half a turn to the front again, then half a turn to the back and so on. The woman maintains her original fall position throughout (Figure 6b).

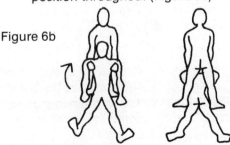

Figure 6b

(c) Man pulls woman in towards him. She turns and falls into a back hand support (Figure 6c).

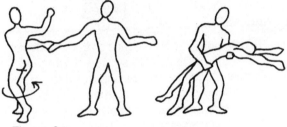

Figure 6c

Many of the 'lean' and 'neck holds' supports mentioned in the previous sections can also begin with a fall.

Standing and Sitting on People

People often worry about stepping, standing or sitting on each other's bodies. If the right part of the body is chosen, however, (usually bone rather than muscle) it should not hurt, and can also be very visually effective. Try choreographing dancers:

(a) Stepping on people stretched out on their stomachs on the floor (step on the lower back).

(b) Standing on a partner's thigh and balancing (Figure 7a).

Figure 7a

(c) Standing with both feet on both thighs (Figure 7b).

Figure 7b

(d) Sitting on someone who is in a crawl position. (The sitter can take his feet off the ground so that his 'human seat' can crawl around (Figure 7c).

Figure 7c

(e) Stepping up a staircase of bodies. Backs must be flat for this. Step rhythmically and quickly on the base of each back (Figure 7d). (This would be delightful for a number such as 'Walk Up the Avenue' (*Easter Parade*).

Figure 7d

Multiple Supports

It can be effective for many couples to perform a sequence of supports in unison. A dance can start or finish with couples performing identical supports or alternatively with a variety of supports and contacts as illustrated in Figure 8. If this idea is used as an opening design, a following transition to unison grouping dancing separately is often exciting.

Lifts

Lifts can be exciting to use on occasions for the sheer fun and novelty value of picking up and putting down bodies! Men can lift other men as well as women!

Technical Hints

A lift is a sensitive act of balance and co-ordination. Various basic guidelines must be followed if lifts are to be successful and injury avoided.

1. It is often easier if the dancer being lifted starts the lift with a preparatory jump. The lifter can, therefore, start lifting his partner when she is higher in the air which eases his task considerably.

2. The couple should synchronise their preparation. Before the jump both partners should bend together and then breathe in simultaneously as the lift commences. It is helpful to give this preparation a rhythmical structure, so as to ensure exactly synchronised timing. If one partner is even a fraction of a second behind the other in the co-ordination of the bend, jump and lift, the lifted person will seem very heavy and the lift itself will lose any sense of ease and flow.

Figure 8

3. The lifter should adopt as broad a base as possible. Generally the feet should be apart and slightly turned out.

4. The lift should finish with a bend so that the dancer does not jar her knees as she lands.

5. Some upwards orientated lifts require the lifter to take a step forward when his partner is in the air so as to get under her.

6. In an upwards lift the man must keep his arms very straight in the air as in weight lifting. Any slight bending will cause undue pain and pressure.

7. The man must be sure of his grip and the position of his hands before attempting the lift. He should be aware of using too much tension - e.g. gripping into a woman's muscle and so causing her pain.

8. The woman must keep her body firm and tense in the air. If she is floppy, she will feel both very heavy and very cumbersome, like a badly packed parcel!

Distribution of weight

The man must ensure that his weight is equally distributed on both feet before the lift starts. The direction of the jump and lift must be clear. In an upwards orientated lift, the girl must jump up as straight as a rocket. Any shift of weight to the side or back will cause a loss of balance and a decrease in directional energy. Any wobbling, fidgeting or adjusting on the part of the woman once she is in the air will have the same effect. Similarly if the man tilts backwards or forwards when lifting, his partner will tend to echo this shift in directional pull and thus the lift will be unsuccessful.

The Aesthetics of Lifts

1. A duo dance should not include too many lifts. Duos are often most effective with a mixture of contacts, touches and supports as well as lifts. A duo dance employing too many lifts will tend to seem laboured and lose ease and flow after a while. A duo with too many lifts can also seem very static. The couple should dance apart for some of the time, sometimes separately, sometimes in canon ensuring that sufficient space is covered. A run into a lift or a travelling lift are ways of achieving this.

2. In a lift, the lifted person should avoid coming down the way she went up! This will only make the lift seem a rather cheap effect as opposed to a logical transition and connection between one movement and the next. Find a logical way of coming out of a lift, one which will ensure a continuity of flow. Come down a different route or continue the lift so that it dissolves into a support or touch.

3. In a 'turning lift' where a man turns or spins a woman around in the air, a sudden loss of momentum can result if the man brings the woman down sharply at the end. This can have a jarring effect, a sudden curtailing of momentum and energy, rather like slamming on the brakes in a car and screeching to a halt. It is possible to overcome this by ensuring that the energy generated by the turn in the air is continued on the floor after the landing. The woman could, for example, continue to run in the same direction as the turning lift for a while when she lands on the floor, perhaps circling around the man, or both partners could immediately travel along a curved pathway.

Examples of Lifts

  *   Easy
 **   More difficult
***   Difficult without good biceps and general practice!

Basic Lifts (Figure 9)

1. *Woman runs towards man and jumps into his arms. She puts her arms round his neck and her legs either side of his body. She hangs on to his neck and he bends forward. He can throw his torso back from this position so that her legs go diagonally up into the air. (Useful in a rock 'n' roll duo) (Figure 9a).

Figure 9a

2. **Woman jumps sideways with a scissor jump kicking her outside then inside leg whilst holding on to the man's shoulder. He holds her in both his arms in the position in which she has arrived, demonstrated in Figure 9b. Using the momentum of the leg kicks she can flick herself over on to her stomach in his arms.

Figure 9b

3. **Man lifts woman straight above him by pushing her up by her outstretched arms. (Her arms must be tense). She can hold her legs out to the side in the air or keep them together. This can be performed with two men each holding one arm (Figure 9c).

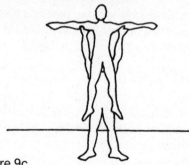

Figure 9c

4. *The seesaw - linking arms, one partner lifts the other on his back. They then change roles repeatedly in quick succession, building up momentum to sustain a regular rhythm in their exchange of weight. Very light people can support very heavy people in this lift due to its basis of momentum (Figure 9d).

Figure 9d

Waist Hold Lifts

A waist hold lift is where the man holds the woman around the waist with both hands. He can either stand directly behind her or facing her. A good preparation for beginners with this sort of lift is the performance of three little jumps. In many waist hold lifts the woman can hold an interesting position with her legs rather than simply keeping them straight and together.

1. ***Man stands behind woman and lifts her above his head. She leans back. He will need to take one step forward to get under her body. This lift can be turned, the lifter gradually bending his arms so that the woman lies over one of his shoulders (Figure 10a)

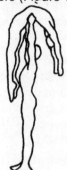

Figure 10a

2. ***Man stands slightly behind the woman. The couple face the audience. Man crosses his arms and puts his hands round the woman's waist and turns her over. It is important to keep the momentum going so that the lifter does not feel the full weight of his partner (Figure 10b).

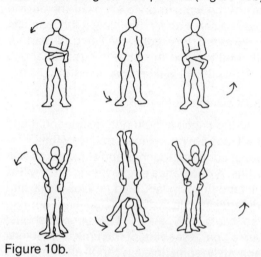

Figure 10b.

Turning Lifts. (See Figure 11)

During turning lifts (particularly with multiple turns) the woman can change her position in the air, curl or uncurl her body in the man's arms for example.

1. **Turning Hug Lifts.* Woman puts her arms round man's neck and bends her knees up by the side of him as he turns her around (see Figure 11a). More simply, the couple may hug, and then the man lift the woman using the same hold. Again the woman will need to tuck her legs up out of the way.

Figure 11a

2. *Woman stretches her arms out to the side and tenses the arm muscles. Man stands behind her and holds her by bending his arms in to support her outstretched arms (see Figure 11b). She can bend up her legs or hold them in a more stretched position (no preparatory jump needed). Or more simply, man may stand behind woman and pick her up by placing his arms around her waist.

Figure 11b

Figure 11c

3. *Man picks up woman by placing one hand under her thigh, the other round her waist and turns her around in the air (no preparatory jump needed) (See Figure 11c).

4. *Flying Aeroplane Lift.* Man holds woman's arm and leg and spins her around very fast (watch the landing!) (See Figure 11d). This would be particularly effective in a number refering to flying e.g. 'Flying Down to Rio' (*Flying Down to Rio*).

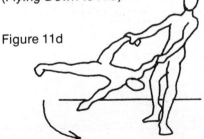

Figure 11d

5. **Partners stand side by side. Man puts arm round woman's waist, whilst she puts an arm round man's back to grip his shoulder. She then jumps up to be held high on his hip and he turns her round. She may bend her legs up or keep them out of the way by bending them (Figure 11e).

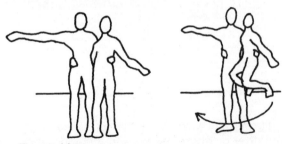

Figure 11e

6. **Man can pull up woman from sitting on the floor into his arms and then turn her around. This should be one phrase of movement.

Travelling Lifts

*Man lifts woman as she performs a step leap. He could hold her on her waist or under her outstretched arms. This is easy to do and highly effective in terms of the delightful increase of height and feeling of suspension. The man must keep up with the woman as she travels by performing rapid small steps by her side. He can direct the jump upwards or along (Figures 12a and b).

Figure 12a

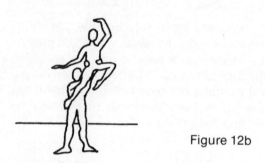

Figure 12b

Lifts With More Than Two Bodies

In group lifts where more than one person lifts another or where one person lifts more than one body, it is usual that the lifted person or people will need to use a preparatory bend and jump before being lifted (as with partner lifts) rather than being 'heaved up'.

1. *The group lifts a dancer using different points of contact (Figure 13a).

Figure 13a

2. *Two men form a seat by crossing their hands. The woman sits on the seat and may use it to swing back and forth, one arm round each of the men (Figure 13b).

Figure 13b

3. **One man lifts two women by holding them around the waist. They can then rest on his thighs (see Figure 13c). This could be used in a number such as 'Two Ladies' from the musical *Cabaret*.

Figure 13c

Canon and Unison Work With Lifts

There is a great sense of energy generated if several couples perform lifts in unison. Or in a group of duos it can be effective to use canon with lifts. The men may pick up the women and turn them round one after another or one man may lift a woman and then put her down for another man to immediately pick her up again and do the same before passing her on to the next man. This activity can even be happening at various places all over the stage.

Other Contact With Duos

a) Ideas with Holding Hands

1. If couples face each other and simply hold hands, there is a lovely sense of clarity and symmetry when the design is duplicated.

2. *Pancake Turns.* Both partners hold both hands facing each other. They then turn inside out without releasing hands and using the same number of steps.

Figure 14a

Figure 14b

3. *Rock 'n' Roll Action.* Partners hold both hands and face each other. They then pull in towards each other, using their biceps, keeping them firm to gather strength and speed. They may then release one hand or push away from each other or perform turns (see Figure 14a).

4. Partners hold both hands (uncrossed) and face each other. One of the couple bends down. Her partner then kicks a leg over her head whilst still holding both hands and performs half a turn to face the opposite direction. He then pulls his partner (who should be sitting on the floor) through his legs, pelvis first, knees together, and rolling in on the feet (see Figure 14b).

5. Man stands behind woman and then puts his arms (one at a time) round her waist and takes hold of both her hands. It is possible to perform travelling steps in unison in this position.

b) Ideas With Different Body Parts in Contact

1. Partners face each other. Partner A places his hands on partner B's shoulders. Partner B places his hands around partner A's waist. They perform turning gallops two to the right, then two to the left.

2. Man holds woman's waist whilst she turns.

3. Man kneels, woman kicks leg over man's hand, then sits on his knee.

4. Man adopts flat back position and places his head on woman's stomach.

5. Man walks backwards and woman forwards whilst maintaining this contact (Figure 15a).

Figure 15a

6. Partners link arms back to back and then collapse to the floor in this position (Figure 15b).

Figure 15b

7. Man holds on to woman's ankles. She turns a half-turn at a time, therefore faces the back, then the front, then the back of the stage. This means that the man rolls over. This is particularly attractive with a number of couples performing it (Figure 15c).

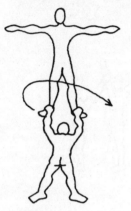

Figure 15c

8. Man and woman place one hand round each other's waist. They both then lean out and turn (Figure 15d).

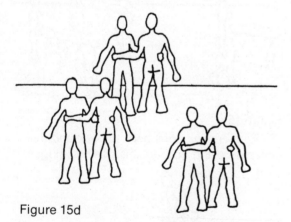

Figure 15d

9. Man and woman hug each other, then pull away from each other whilst maintaining the arm positions they had in the hug.

10. More unusual contacts are exciting, for example a hand on a partner's head, or a knee against a partner's thigh.

Comic Effects With Body Contact

1. *'Buddah' Effects.* The 'Buddah' effect is one where two or more bodies purposely merge to be one being by standing very close, usually one behind the other, so that it is difficult to tell which body parts belong to whom. Arms and legs can appear and move as if they belong to the front person. In Figure 16a the arms of the two people move in the opposite directions. Then the A's move to the B's position and vice versa. In Figure 16b the movement is more

Figure 16a

random and flowing. The woman may sit in between the man's legs and do the same as him. In Figure 16c the girl in front is bending towards the man behind her therefore her legs become his! Figure 16d shows a 'Buddah'

Figure 16b   Figure 16c

effect with more than two people, whilst in Figure 16e a man keeps peering out from behind his partner.

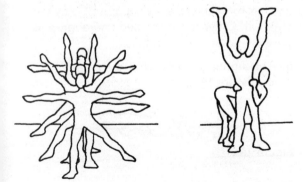

Figure 16d   Figure 16e

2. Other humorous uses of body contact can be to choreograph monsters, or people with large body extensions of some sort, dancing with normal sized humans. It can be comical to see how and where they hold on to each other. Or performers may dance with invisible partners (using a ballroom hold of course) or dance with a mop, broom, umbrella or hatstand as their partner. Performers can use other people's limbs in more unusual ways. For example, one person may play another person's leg as if it were a guitar, or take a bite out of it as if it were a loaf of French bread! (see Figure 16f). Try couples jumping together in a

Figure 16f

hug with arms around each other's neck, and travelling in this position from one side of the stage to the other. In Figure 16g one person can run and jump into a line of people (scaring to do at first but safe). The group may then lift

the body above their heads and run around the stage with it. This can be even more comical if the person held up above seems to be quite at ease up there, reclining back, giving someone a call on the telephone, or eating grapes (see Figure 16g). It can be very amusing to have various groups all using this method of transportation simultaneously.

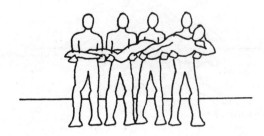

Figure 16g.

3. *Body Buildings* (Figure 17). Dancers can be grouped together using physical contact to create a building of some sort. Another group can then use this structure:

a) The Human Wall - Dancers can walk along the top of it.

b) The Climbing Frame - Dancers can play on it, move through it, stand on it.

c) The Human Couch - A dancer can lie on it. The couch may be composed of several bodies kneeling together with flat back or one body as shown in Figure 17a.

Figure 17a

d) The Human Chair - A dancer can be carried on it, or just sit in it.

e) The Human Tunnel - Dancers can crawl through it.

Figure 17b

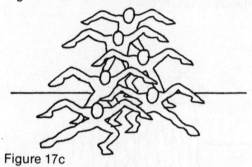

Figure 17c

Other human buildings are not suitable for supporting other dancers but instead can be used to emphasise the particular togetherness of a group, as shown in Figures 17b and c.

4. *The Human Heap.* The floor heap can either be organised, one body lying neatly across another (arrived at in canon) or a more random arrangement as shown in Figure 18a. Alternatively, there is the raised or walking heap where one torso rests over another (see Figure 18b). This would be appropriate for the 'doomed' group or the prisoners.

Figure 18a

Figure 18b

5. *Fights and Physical Aggression* (Figure 19) Fighting or any show of anger is most convincing when a lot of energy is expended. High jumps, fast turns, leaping on and off furniture and throwing chairs, are all appropriate by this criterion. Other more detailed choreographic possibilities are outlined below:

a) The fighting couple roll over each other (Figure 19a).

Figure 19a

b) The aggressor punches out at his victim which develops into a double spin whilst the victim ducks (Figure 19b).

Figure 19b

c) The aggressor and victim stand side by side. The aggressor then pulls the victim in front of her body (joining left hands in front of the body) which results in the victim performing a long sequence of spins.

d) The aggressor performs acrobatic jumps over his partner as if to throw his body at his victim. He then performs a somersault to ease the fall.

e) The victim falls back into the aggressor's arms, who then pushes him to the side. This causes the victim to roll along the floor several times.

f) The aggressor jumps on the victim's back in order to pull him to the floor, but the victim simply walks around with the aggressor on his back who in turn madly throws his arms around in the air in frustration.

g) One man throws himself at a group, who all fall down.

A comic effect to conclude a bout of heavy aggressive fighting may be simply to push the aggressor in the chest with a delicate staccato gesture of one finger. This slight touch could be enough to make the aggressor wobble and fall over. The 'walking torso lean' is a delightful preliminary to a fight to demonstrate the exchange of power. The couple face each other. One walks backwards, the other forwards, with the rhythm one-two/one-two-three, then they change and walk the other way. Eye contact and a straight torso lean must be maintained throughout.

6. *Simulated Strangulation.* As with all other literal gestures used in a dance context, strangulation should be exaggerated. The strangler could, for example, hold his victim around the neck and shake him. The victim may respond by shaking the whole of his body and performing little running steps on the spot to emphasise this.

7. *Crowd Fights.* It can be effective for several couples to perform a fighting dance in unison. If the 'biffs' and 'punches' are performed with fast tempoed and syncopated rhythms, such an event can be difficult to polish. To find out where inaccuracies lie, therefore, rehearse the 'victims' and 'aggressors' separately for a while, before reuniting in rehearsal with their partners.

Personal Body Contact and Body Noise

The dancer can hold or touch part of his own body. Such contact is often particularly appropriate for character study and the humorous situation. Paranoia and obsessive behaviour often manifest themselves in fidgeting by con-

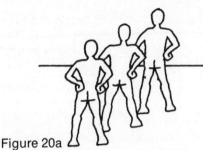

Figure 20a

tact with the body. Such contact can also create very clear and novel spatial designs as illustrated in Figure 20a and b. Other examples

Figure 20b

are demonstrated in Figure 21. In Figure 22 the joined hands in front of the body act as a delightful contrast to the angularity of the legs. An effective transition is one where the dancer starts with some contact with his own body and then adopts a totally open and peripheral position.

Figure 21

Figure 22

Body Noise, Slaps and Claps

Body noise can raise energy level and generate excitement as well as providing aural accompaniment to the dance. Take for example the 'Schulplattler' idea, a dance centering around hand contact with the thighs:

1. Slap left thigh with left hand
2. Slap right thigh with right hand
3. Slap left foot with right hand
4. Clap both hands in the air
5. Clap both hands under right knee

High claps above the head are pleasing visually and aurally. Try performing these with a syncopated rhythm:

clap clap clap slap thighs slap thighs clap slap
  1 and 2   3   and 4   5 and 6

A line of dancers facing sideways and clapping shows the delightful profile of the clapping gesture.

Eye Contact

Eye contact between two dancers on stage can be very effective and expressive. The spectator often refers to eye contact between performers in order to gather information about the nature of the relationship, whether for example one performer is sending angry or affectionate messages to another. Sometimes distance with eye contact conveys more emotional warmth between two people than proximity with no eye contact. Eye contact during approach and withdrawal is also an important way of establishing the nature of a relationship, whether for example there is intimacy, apprehension or annoyance. Consider carefully whether an approach should happen from behind, from the side, or head on. Should the partners look at each other or does one turn away? Is the approaching walk fast and even with an upright body or is it a 'crouched sneaking'?

5. Groupings and Designs

The grouping of dancers gives a sense of order and makes it easier for the audience to understand a musical. Such grouping can help the spectator to see distinctions between characters and identify new events and people more quickly. Decisions about grouping include considerations of how to choreograph formations, floor patterns and of the distance to have between members of a group or between co-existing groups.

There is a useful distinction between formal and naturalistic grouping. Naturalistic grouping can be seen in a 'gathering' or 'cluster' where there is no stress on tidy equidistance or precise duplication of shape. People stand randomly, as a group of individuals all of whom have their own body shape, design, level and direction of focus. Formal grouping, however, has greater regularity in arrangement, more common elements in terms of shape, level and direction and thus a greater sense of repetition and symmetry. Formal grouping is appropriate where the dancers have the same personalities, reactions or identity whereas naturalistic grouping can convey the diversity of characters and their reactions to a situation. The formal group often lacks human connotations because in real life (except perhaps at weddings or funerals) people rarely stand like this. However, the formal group is very easy for the eye to take in and thus is appropriate when an immediate impact is required. This is why it is often very effective to use a formal group for the opening number of a show: the members of the chorus acting as a unified group.

General Tips about Choreographic Grouping

1. *Simplicity.* In the choreography of musicals (unlike other forms of theatre dance) there is a particular tension between the visual and the auditory because of the presence of sung words. If a particular grouping is highly complex the spectator may need to give it his full attention thus detracting from his ability to understand the lyrics. It is never the job of choreography to push another element of the musical into second place and accordingly it must be kept more simple than the subtle spatial patternings of contemporary or ballet dance. Musicals demand the *obvious*, the *clear*, the *symmetrical*, the *regular*, and the *immediately identifiable*.

1. *Environmental Considerations.* Choreographic simplicity is also important when a stage is cluttered with scenery and props. It is unusual for the choreographer of a musical to have the luxury of a bare stage and the effects of complex linear body designs may be lost against a background of interplaying lines, curves and shapes belonging to the setting. The choreographer therefore needs to be fully aware of his working environment when planning the grouping, because the set design may well contain shapes which conflict with, or destroy the lines of the choreography. For example, a set which contains many curves may reduce the effects of a very angular choreographic design. In addition, the choreographer should take careful note of the surrounding proportions. A set with a great sense of height and majestic proportions may have the effect of reducing the dancers to little more than insignificant miniatures and may have to be counterbalanced by placing them on a higher level such as a set of rostra or a balcony.

Distance between Group Members and between Groups

1. *The Significant Gap.* The choreographer should establish the most pleasing and appropriate distance between members of a group and between groups. Sometimes this may

seem an intuitive process. He may simply 'know' that a gap needs enlarging or closing as we do when arranging objects on a shelf. (Perhaps such judgments are based on our previous knowledge of, and associations with, certain spatial relationships between living things.) Variance in spatial gaps can suggest such feelings as attraction, repulsion, intimacy, being trapped, isolation, loneliness, intrusion, tension, invasion, imprisonment or such concepts as balance, contrast, expansion, distance, unity, dispersal, segregation, separation and containment. As a choreographer you must be aware of such considerations when deciding how two or more individuals or groups are to be juxtaposed. Too little regard for spatial gaps may lead to ambiguity of meaning so you must spend time experimenting with group members being close to each other and then further apart. Consider the appropriateness of the spacing both in terms of the intended meaning and the actual movements and costumes being used. Pay attention also to the spatial relationships not only between people and groups but to the empty space which surrounds them. Choreography avoids visual monotony by there being variation in spaces between one dancer and another (see Figures 1a and b). Naturally, there are some exceptions to this, for example when a formation dance depends on a state of continued equidistance throughout.

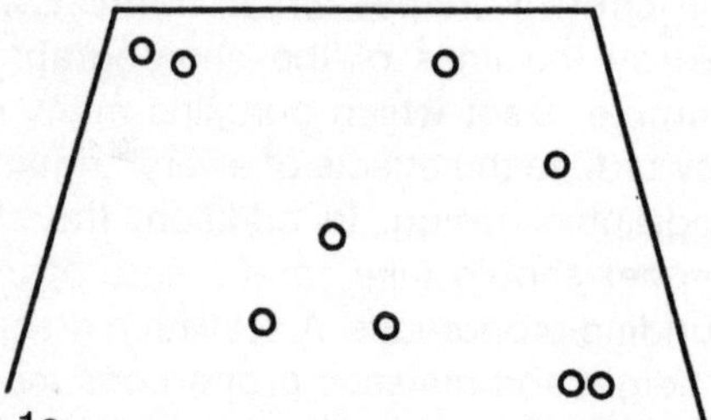

2. *'Too Close' Grouping.* Groups or members of a group who are too close together can produce 'interference'. Some body designs appear sharp and well-defined in isolation but lose their impact when used in a close group together. The design in Figure 2 is spatially

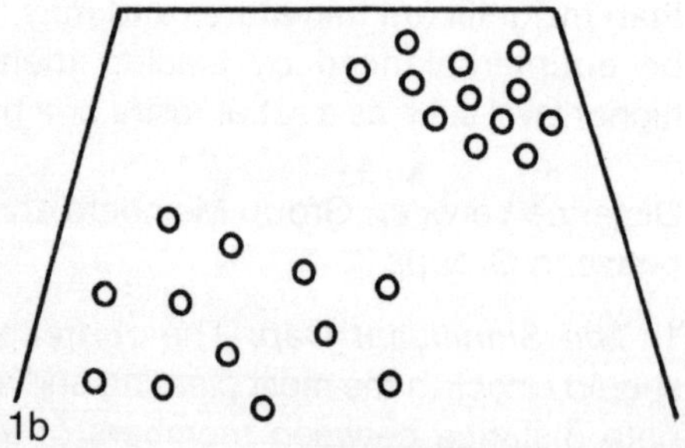

Figure 2

very clear but if the dancers are too close together the result is an ill-defined mass. A complex, asymmetrical body design such as is shown Figure 3 also demands a more distanced grouping.

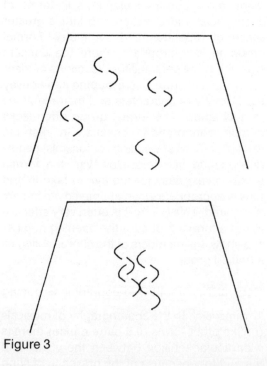

Figure 1a

Figure 1b

Figure 3

Problems of closeness often result from a stage having to accommodate more performers than it can comfortably hold and with repeated grouping, for example, it is wise to question whether there is some unnecessary duplication. Aim for the highest level of interest which the repetition can provide, whilst avoiding redundancies and over-crowding. The repeated cluster designs in Figure 4 illustrate the choices which the choreographer is likely to have to face. It is difficult to generalise, but on an average size stage, say 40 ft. by 30 ft. (12 metres by 9 metres) and with energetic and spacious choreography, there should be no more than eight to twelve people dancing if they are to remain comfortably equidistant. This number of dancers provides a feeling of fullness without over-crowding (Figure 5).

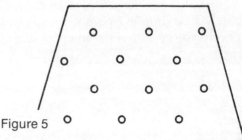

Figure 5

Other problems caused by over-closeness are masking and restlessness. In the initial stages of choreography a gap can seem wide enough to avoid masking and yet from certain viewpoints in the auditorium a dancer may in fact be masked by another. Figure 6 shows an example of this where from seat X dancer A will appear masked although she is distinctly to the side of B. This underlines the importance of checking grouping from all possible angles.

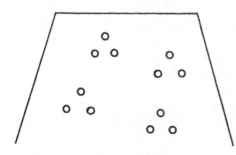

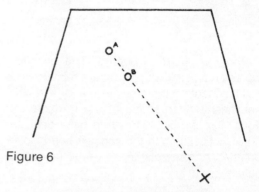

Figure 6

Figure 7 shows two people standing very close to each other and this apparent invasion of space may produce a sensation of restlessness both in performers and audience.

It is, of course, vital that the performers themselves realise the importance of precision in spatial positioning, including the width of the gaps set, and do not simply regard such

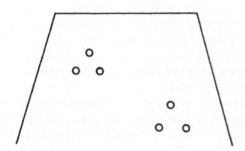

Figure 4

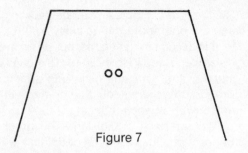

Figure 7

precision as the over-fussiness of the choreo-grapher. As we show in Figure 8, the smallest shift in position can break the entire tension of a design.

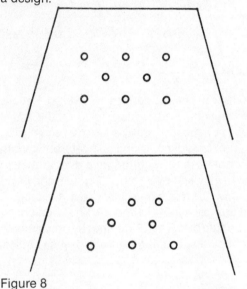

Figure 8

3. *'Too Far Apart' Grouping*. The overwide gap can result in grouping where relationships are indefinable; it is difficult to see for example, that the intended shape of the formation in Figure 9 is a wedge: it would have been far more successful had the dancers been closer together. An over-distanced group leads to a

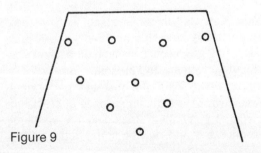

Figure 9

loose sense of boundary, a loss in visual strength, and a tendency for the stage to appear uncomfortably empty. Furthermore, certain body shapes and gestures become less obvious and easily lost in too much space; the isolated movement of clenching and unclen-ching of a fist, for example, may pass unnoticed or simply be interpreted as fidgeting if the var-ious members of a group carrying out the action are six feet apart.

4. *Effects and Advantages of a Variety of Gaps*

The Close Group

The close group can provide a visually satis-fying compactness; by its clear sense of boun-dary it can introduce an element of tidyness to a perhaps otherwise cluttered stage. Audience attention may therefore be attracted by the immediately apparent sense of order of the close group: its visual clarity emphasises the idea of group membership, particularly if the dancers are equidistant from each other. A spatially extreme version of the close group is the 'clump'. In this formation, as illustrated in Figure 10, the gaps between dancers are hardly noticable. Overlapping may be intro-duced to further the sense of proximity. The

Figure 10

clump is particularly suited to stationary move-ment or to travelling with tiny shuffling steps. Its particular tidyness can be emphasised by using fast directional changes and small iso-lated gestures such as a sharp raising and lowering of the shoulders, a quick flick of the hand, a turn of the head or a drop of the torso. Moreover, the clump's clear boundary line makes it possible for other groups to be on stage at the same time without resulting in interference or visual confusion. This is particularly appropriate for performers who are exact equivalents whether in terms of role, costume, status or personality.

The Distant Group

The distant group is a useful device to provide an effect of a full stage or of a crowd scene, particularly if the dancers are performing expansive and energetic movements. The group can appear larger if the performers are positioned in such a way that the crowd appear to extend off stage. The distant group is also appropriate when the choreographer wishes to convey that the group members have little in common and would, in reality, not choose to stand next to each other. The plot may determine that these people share the same environment but are little more than strangers together. It is rarely a good idea for dancers wearing very different costumes to be positioned in a close group because this sets up an ambiguity between the costume and choreographic design. On occasions it may prove successful to choreograph a situation where, because of a sudden disagreement or moment of shock, a close and regularly shaped group breaks up to establish a more random grouping. Such transition and the mode of separation can be very exciting.

The Equidistant Group

Equidistance is an arrangement of identical intervals between one group member and the next. The effect is often one of order, balance and regularity. Problems can arise when travelling as a group in keeping the exact distances first established; this requires a high degree awareness and concentration on the part of each group member for it is all too easy to catch up with the next person (a concertina effect) or to enlarge the distances. Figure 11 illustrates a very popular equidistant spacing for musicals where the dancers in each line stand in the gaps created by the dancers just in front of them.

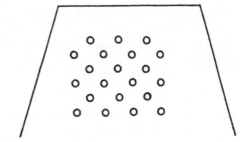

Figure 11

Positions on Stage

The choreographer must recognise that there are powerful and weak areas on a stage, powerful and weak pathways, entrances and exits. The word 'weak' here is not used in a pejorative sense and at times it may be desirable to use the weak areas. For example, groups might be placed in such weaker areas to avoid competition with a group which needed to be noticed immediately. Similarly, a weak entrance is appropriate for a character who wishes to creep on stage during a moment of great activity without drawing attention to his or herself or detracting attention from a major event taking place on another part of the stage. It is important to explore and exploit the potential of areas and pathways in terms of their relative power, in order to provide the clearest possible communication of ideas and themes; we must therefore consider these issues now.

a) Front of the Stage

This tends to be a 'warm' area because it is close to the audience and is particularly suitable for any dance number expressing a warm or life-affirming emotion; the humorous dance or love duet, for example. Great sensitivity is needed here and to avoid embarassment or a sense of voyeurism the intimate expression of love in a duo may be best placed a little further back. On the other hand, scenes concerning busy activity or frenetic energy or even panic benefit by being placed as near to the front of the stage as possible. Rather as telegraph poles appear to flick past from the window of a train, so the nearer we are to the action the greater the illusion of speed. Finally, it must be remembered that the corners of the front of the stage (i.e. Downstage Right and Left on a proscenium stage) are weaker areas than the centre.

b) Centre Stage

This is potentially a very powerful position although it is important that it should not be over used. It may serve as a focal point or as an ordering device. In Figure 12, for example, the central group is regularly formed which helps the spectator to see the more dispersed and random activity surrounding it more clearly. The central wedge here acts as a balance, a stabiliser, a contrast and a focal point.

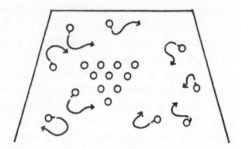

Figure 12

c) Back of the Stage

This area, known as Upstage traditionally, is an area of great atmosphere sometimes enhanced by the set design. The centre back and the two centre corners are particularly strong areas; for example, the position upstage left is sometimes known as 'Rothbart's corner' after the character Rothbart in *Swan Lake* who epitomises evil and who manifests his power in spasmodic appearances from this corner and uses the diagonal pathway to downstage right.

The remoteness of the back of the stage is ideal for evoking a sense of mystery either about the place itself or its inhabitants and can suggest intrigue and darkness. When characters are positioned all over the stage, those further back will tend to appear dominant.

d) Sides of the Stage

Side areas and pathways from one side to another tend to be weak. Events taking place in these areas are often missed or seen as having less importance, especially when competing with happenings in more central positions. The centre sides are particularly weak. When using side positions, it is important to be aware of the spatial intervals between the dancers and the edge of the stage: a dancer placed too near the side, as shown in Figure 13, is potentially 'restless' and will convey a sense of tension to the audience. A similar effect results from a group or a dancer being slightly off-centre.

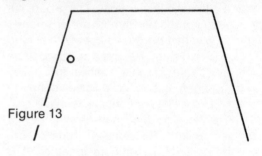

Figure 13

To clarify weak and strong positions refer to Figure 14. Weak positions and pathways are drawn with wiggly lines and strong with straight lines.

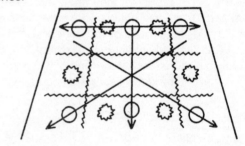

Figure 14

Levels

Variation in level can be achieved either by altering the position of the body or by using items of stage furniture such as rostra, ramps or balconies. Both methods are equally valid and each has particular advantages. In each case the object is to provide depth, height, perspective and interest. Variation in level may also solve problems of masking.

Differences in the design of various groups are often more easily noticed with the use of several levels, but it is especially important to give attention to the precise mode and timing of transition from one level to another. It is often most effective to bring about a level change gradually. If, by contrast, a large number of the cast suddenly jump from a high level to the ground, the effect is comic rather than impressive and will provide the audience with a problem of readjustment to a spectacle that has unexpectedly lost all its height and variety! A stage can often accommodate many groups without the problems of merging, interference or loss of separation if each group is provided with its own, distinct level.

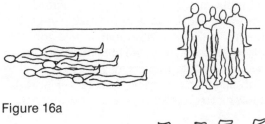

Figure 16a

a) Body Levels

Kneeling, sitting, lying or standing (lower by bending the knees or higher by rising onto the balls of the feet), lifts and falls are all ways of using the body to gain a variety of level. In Figure 15, for example, the arm motif is com-

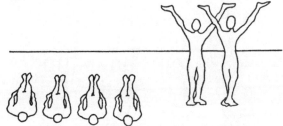

Figure 16b

b) Bobbing Up and Down

A sudden change of level brought about when certain members of a group quickly adopt a lower position to that of their co-members can be very exciting (see Figure 17a, b, & c). Figure 18 shows bobbing up and down on a row basis

Figure 15

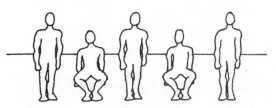

Figure 17a

Figure 17b

mon to all the dancers but the level is varied. Bodies lying on the floor can be especially effective if they are placed next to people standing up. Lying down can look very tidy if used with an absence of arm gestures as in Figure 16a & b. In such cases, as with other variations in level, the choreographer might emphasise difference in status between the characters.

Figure 17c

and the effect of this can be increased if accompanied by an unpredictable rhythmic change on, say, beat one, beat five and beat eleven. Alternatively, the change may be even less ordered; individuals may simply appear to bob up and down at random as in Figure 19. Slow motion level change is also very attractive.

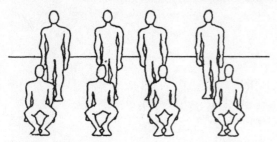

Figure 18

Most devices for change of level are, in fact, simple but effective: these include rising onto the ball of the foot and lowering again (particularly pleasing when performed 'staccato') and, of course, the simple bending of the knees!

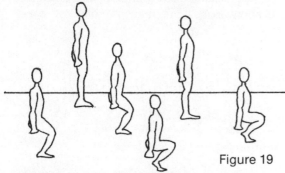

Figure 19

c) Using the Levels of the Set

Just as it is necessary to exploit the full depth and width of the stage it is also important to use its height. Various levels integral to the setting may be used in conjunction with body levels to achieve a dynamic stage image (see Figures 20 and 21).

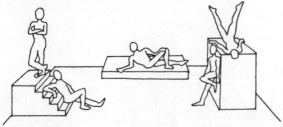

Figure 20

Figure 21

Directions and Where to Face

Throughout this section we shall be using a number of symbols and floor plans adapted from Labanotation. These were originally orientated from the dancer's viewpoint. However, as this book is for choreographers, we have reversed their orientation.

⊓ facing front (audience)

⊞ facing stage left

⊟ facing stage right

⊔ facing up stage

As with levels, it is vital not to be limited choreographically by failing to exploit fully the excitement of changes in direction and the use of multiple directions. It is a common fault of novice choreographers to over-use the 'front-on' direction and force performers to face the audience directly throughout every dance. This is a legacy of the Busby Berkley era of musicals when it was the accepted thing for large, regimented choruses to dance smiling out at the audience, an effect which now seems both brash and banal. Facing front is undeniably an excellent means of gaining contact with the audience, exuding warmth, projecting sound and conveying both energy and openness. After a while, however, the flatness loses its appeal and the more attractive possibilities of facing side or back and of exploiting diagonals must be explored.

Facing the Side

Facing sideways brings into prominence a variety of body designs: many torso, hip and shoulder movements are displayed to the most advantage in this position. Figure 22 demonstrates this, whereas Figures 23 and 24 show how a sideways angle uses a linear formation effectively. Additionally, various forms of physical contact can be best seen from the side

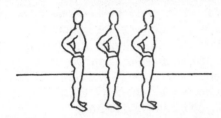

Figure 22

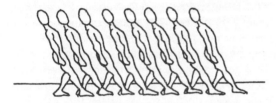

Figure 23

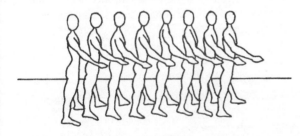

Figure 24

(see Figure 25). Obviously it must be remembered that only half of the body can be seen from the side so two-arm designs, for example,

Figure 25

may be redundant. Figure 26 shows a body design for which sideways orientation would be a bad choice. However, it is always possible

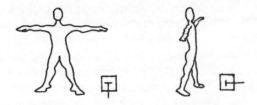

Figure 26

to overcome the problem of the 'hidden limb' by making it visible by other means. The back arm, for example, can be lifted as in Figures 27 and 28 or, alternatively, obscured body parts

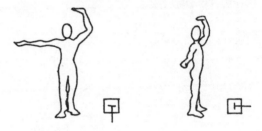

Figure 27

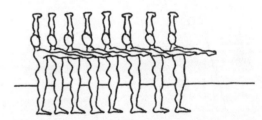

Figure 28

can be turned in isolation towards the audience whilst the rest of the body keeps its sideways orientation (Figure 29).

Figure 29

Facing the Diagonal

A group of performers or even individuals appear visually very strong when facing a diagonal or moving along a diagonal pathway. The pathway from upstage right to downstage left is often considered the strongest of all and is thus associated with a climax or a crescendo (see Figure 30). Striking effects can be achieved by unison groups positioned either very close or far apart all of whom adopt positions in which the main point of focus is the diagonal but with some body parts facing a contrasting direction. A good example of this would be where the whole body is orientated on the diagonal but the upper torso and head face front.

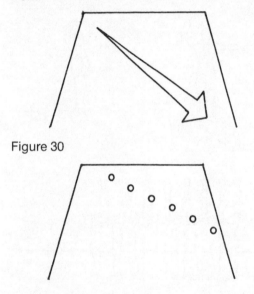

Figure 30

Naturally 'polishing' a diagonal-facing group can be time consuming, because it is very difficult for dancers to orientate themselves correctly on a diagonal without very precise instructions. It is easy for performers to imagine that the whole body is facing the same diagonal when in fact there is some degree of twisting in the hips so that the lower part of the body is on a different diagonal from the head and shoulders. The best way to overcome this problem is for the performers to focus on the same distant object and to orientate themselves spatially from the hip bones so that their shoulders are directly above the hip bones.

Once the hips and shoulders are correctly placed, the rest of the body will follow.

Facing back

Provided that they are not attempting to sing as well, it is perfectly acceptable for performers to dance with their backs toward the audience. Used without arm gestures, the back facing position can be an extremely powerful linear design with none of the distractions of the front of the body. The torso is displayed clearly and cleanly.

At the opening of a dance, backs to the audience can be a most effective way of introducing a group of new and unfamiliar characters. Their sudden turn to face the front, especially if combined with a burst of singing or the revelation of startling masks or facial make-up, can be highly dramatic. Conversely, facing the back can be a useful device for reducing the attention paid to a particular group without their having to actually leave the stage; a chorus may even freeze with their backs to the audience and almost blend into the set whilst, say, some secret assignation between the two main characters takes place downstage (Figure 31).

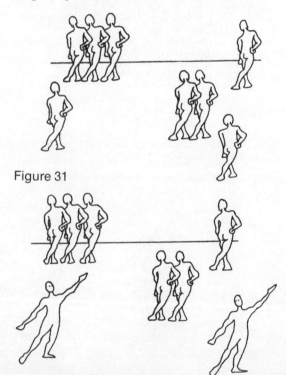

Figure 31

A good deal of time may be necessary to 'polish' a turn from back to front or vice versa as it is essential that the turn occurs on a precise beat and in exact unison.

Mixed Facings

Groups whose members are facing in various directions can be visually attractive, particularly if the groups themselves differ in other ways. In Figure 32, for example, the two groups differ not only in the direction they face

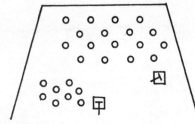

Figure 32

but also in the distance between members and the size of the group. Figure 33 shows an interesting variation in direction where the action is upstage centre, a middle group is watching the action (backs to the audience) and another group is downstage left commenting on the

Figure 33

action to the audience. Figure 34 shows the chaotic effect where there is disparity within one group, perhaps in a situation of disaster or despair.

Figure 34

A slightly different version would result if all the heads were choreographed to be turned in the same direction whilst the rest of the body alone conveys the chaos and confusion of events. Figure 35a, b, & c shows other effects which may be achieved by mixed facings.

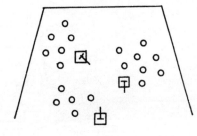

Figure 35a

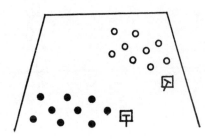

Figure 35b

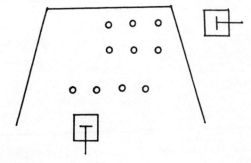

Figure 36c

Changes of Direction

Sudden directional changes in a group, particularly as part of a travelling pattern, are usually exciting and interesting because of the level of unpredictability and skill involved. The effect is heightened if the group moves in unison and performs a succession of such changes. The staccato quality of direction change can be emphasised by turning the head slightly before the rest of the body, thereby changing the visual focus of the group. Figures 36 and 37 show examples of direction change.

Figure 36

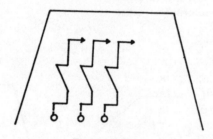

Figure 37

6. Regular Formations

'Regular' will be taken to describe any formation which is easily classifiable and identifiable as opposed to an irregular shape which may have odd protrusions or jutting sections. Thus a regular formation will include the line, circle or square.

The Single Line

The line is a simple, very noticeable formation even if placed within a rather chaotic environment; this is clearly shown in the selection of pathways in Figure 1. The line can be used as a device for attracting the spectator's attention and is often most effective with equidistant spacing and unison movement. Lines are excellent to display the virtuosity, precision foot work and energy of the trio, quartet or quintet although, of course, one of the classic dance formations is the long line of chorus girls. An example of the type of sequence which can be performed by a line of five is given below: note that it includes the use of the various directions discussed in the previous chapter and is best performed with staccato changes:

1. Three steps forward   **ALWAYS**
2. Two steps to the right   **MOVING**
3. Two steps to the back   **THE**
4. Three steps to face the front **FEET**
5. Two steps to face the left side **RIGHT**
6. One step to the back   **THEN**
7. One step to face the left side **LEFT**
8. Three steps to face the front.

Problems do, however occur from the over-use of the line; the over-static and generally frontal activity can quickly become boring; its original attractive simplicity can soon dissolve into a sense of monotony. Some choreographers aggravate the situation by the use of

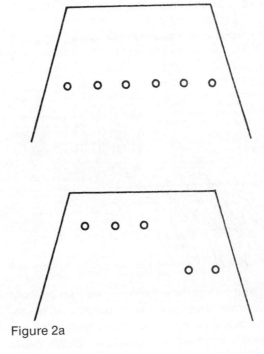

Figure 2a

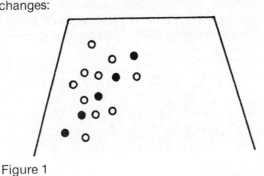

Figure 1

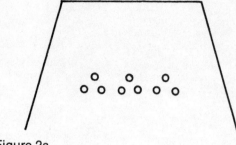

Figure 2a

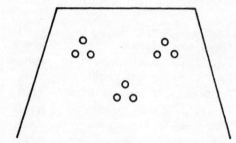

Figure 2b

insufficient depth in their groupings with the result that dancers in originally separate groups become part of a line unintentionally! The illustrations here show how such errors can be avoided and visual interest maintained; Figure 2a & b demonstrates that by splitting up a line and placing some performers more up and downstage, monotony is overcome. Figures 3,

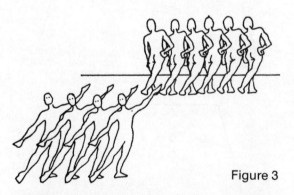

Figure 3

4, and 5 show how various lines can co-exist on stage and how juxtapositions of sexes, directional facing or movement sequences can greatly increase the dynamism of the visual

effect. There is a whole range of possibilities of the variations between As and Bs within a group, alternate members may, for example, wear different costumes or sing and remain silent.

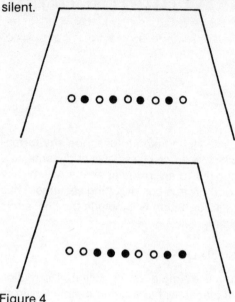

Figure 4

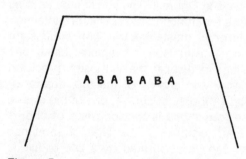

A B A B A B A

Figure 5

Physical Contact in a Line

Physical contact emphasises the sense of togetherness: Figure 6 shows a group linking arms whilst they perform a complex stepping

Figure 6

pattern and move sideways; Figure 7 shows a group moving as one body because there is no gap between one member and the next; this grouping is particularly appropriate for seductive situations where the group displays hip and shoulder movements with the head facing front. Waist joining can also form the basis of dragon or snake scenes where there is much spiralling and tail-lashing.

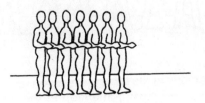

Figure 7

Figure 8 shows a flat torso line which lends itself to all manner of hip wiggling and bottom shaking as well as head rolling and Figure 9

Figure 8

illustrates how one constantly turning dancer can be passed along a line, a device which can be most effective if the group members show some reaction, such as affection or dislike towards the moving dancer. Members of a close line may fall back into each other's arms in ripple canon until they are all on the floor and this will add to a sense of shock or clowning.

Figure 9

Moving in the Line

Changing places: Figure 10 shows how each alternate person in a line can change places by moving into the next space to their right. The As perform first, then the Bs follow suit.

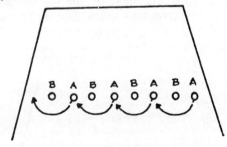

Figure 10

Splitting: Figure 11a & b shows how one line may split into two by alternate members moving back or out to the side.

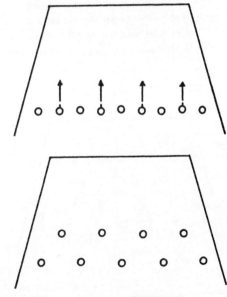

Figure 11a

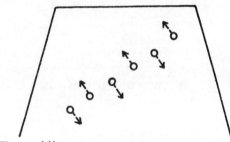

Figure 11b

Dosy Do: it is usual for dosy do to be done facing your partner but it can be performed with both partners keeping a front-on orientation. Both dancers face the front throughout. They simply change places by the dancer at the back moving forwards and the dancer at the front moving backwards, passing by opposite shoulders respectively.

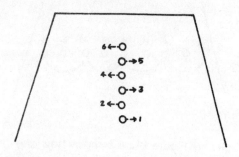

Figure 12

Jumping Out: in Figure 12 members in the line jump out to the side one by one in ripple canon. Transition *into* a line can be achieved from many formations and is illustrated in Figure 13.

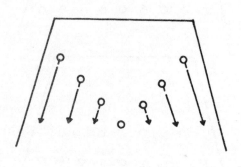

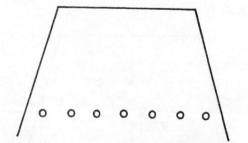

Figure 13

Canon in a Line: this can be very effective if movements are performed in quick succession, one movement overlapping the time phrase of the next. It can be laborious if performed slowly, especially if a slight gap is left between each movement (Figure 14).

Figure 14

Comedy in the Line: the line can be a useful device for drawing attention to the 'odd one out' or misfit (Figure 15).

Figure 15

Double Line and Procession: the clarity of the double line with all its sinuous qualities and possibilities is well exploited in the danced procession (Figure 16). If there are very few people to create the illusion of a large procession then it is necessary to leave large gaps between one couple and the next and before each couple enters the stage. Dancers may

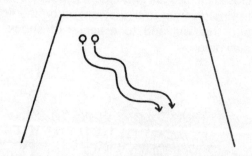

Figure 16

also peel off from the double line to form a block as illustrated in Figure 17: this can provide a fitting conclusion to a procession such as the one in 'I'm a Brass Band' (*Sweet Charity*) and 'When the Parade Passes By (*Hello Dolly*). The procession can also split

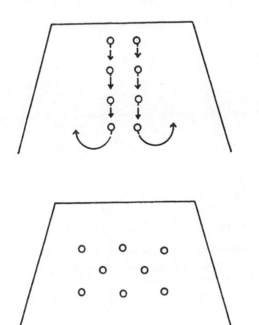

Figure 17

and cross as in Figure 18. A double line can be used for a comic procession to symbolise a vehicle such as a train as in *42nd Street* or a coach and horses as in *Oliver*. Members of the group can either represent the vehicle, the passengers or both; outside members can easily create 'wheel' effects with 'chug chug' circles of the arms.

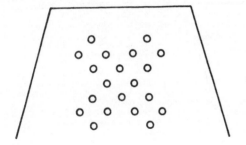

Figure 18

The Circle

The circle is a formation to be treated with caution and discretion: its basic symmetry means that it has no spatial tension and may have such associations as primitive ritual or children's games for the spectator. Where an inner focusing circle is used in a dance the spectator may feel excluded as his field of vision makes it impossible for him to have the same view as a member of that circle. Such problems, of course, are avoided if the staging is in the round or if the audience seating is raked around a thrust stage so that the floor patterns of circles are totally visible to the audience.

The complexity and tension lacking within a single circle can, to some extent, be re-established by introducing a number of circles. A very attractive effect will result from the interlinking of such circles when travelling in opposite directions (see Figure 19). Outward facing

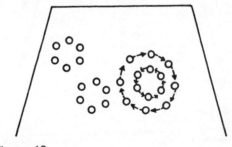

Figure 19

circles are another device which gives visual impact to a stage, and the choreographer should experiment with various directions of travel. Figure 20 illustrates an exciting possibility where a solo performer travels in and out of circles and it is possible to create a tremendous sense of tension if two performers

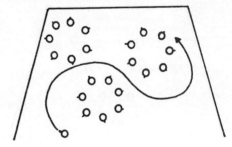

Figure 20

chase between revolving circles. Extra energy can be generated by acceleration, and added interest will result by placing a circle next to a different formation. It may sometimes be advantageous to use the circle formation only momentarily before it opens out into a line.

The Curved and Spiral Formation

The curved or spiral formation and floor pattern often has a greater sense of movement than the straight line. A semicircle often suggests warmth, comfort and compassion, in comparison to the coldness and formality of the straight line which is arguably more suited to virtuoso display than to the expression of emotion. Figure 21 shows how a semicircle may be used as a frame to accommodate another group.

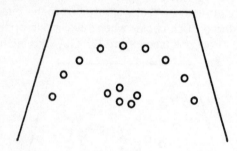

Figure 21

The Wedge

The wedge is a very appealing and frequently used formaton for musicals: it carries the inherent strengths of diagonal lines and their points of merger and is both more interesting and provides fewer masking problems than the square. Choreographers can exploit the

change of leaders from one line to another and will find the formation particularly useful when a display of symmetrical movement is needed. The open 'V' as illustrated in Figure 22a is probably most effective for showing a succession of directional changes and Figure 22b shows some of the transitional possibilities.

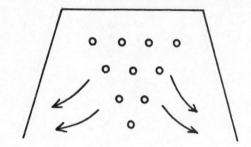

Figure 22b

Formations and the Use of Space Specifically for the Solo, Duo, Trio and Quartet

The number of people in a group will define and limit to some extent what is possible both spatially and bodily. It is important to keep the spectator's interest by changing the numbers in the subdivisions of a group from time to time. For example, a group of six should be subdivided to form groups of four and two, or three and three, or even three two and a soloist, in order to exploit fully the potential of the sextet. The table on page 81 sets out all the possible subgroupings of various groups: it deals specifically with small sized groups as these lend themselves to sharp directional changes, body isolations and more complex stepping patterns.

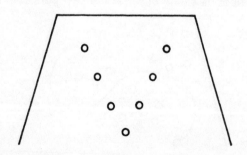

Figure 22a

THE SPATIAL POSSIBILITIES OF DIFFERENT NUMERICAL GROUPS

	Dramatic Ideas	Direction, Formation & Amount of Space	Numerical Possibilities & Movement Ideas
o	Isolation Freedom Intimate sharing with the Spectator (The solo can often arouse a high level of spectatorial sympathy)	Be aware of the solo figure being 'marooned' in too much space. Sometimes it is preferable to position the soloist next to some part of the set or near to another group for some or all of the dance, to provide a frame or context.	Any form of travelling - running, jumping, etc. General spatial exploration
o	Leaving Parting Confronting Avoiding Attacking Meeting	The duo can be effective either staying on the spot or using a lot of space. Avoid duos that never use the depth of the stage where partners stand side by side (see Figure 23) Duos can be danced with the partners facing each other, but are often better orientated towards the audience, however emotionally close the relationship is.	Crossing; Dosy do; Passing by (2 together or 1 + 1) Double duo work is highly attractive (see Figure 24) All coexisting duos can perform the same movements but their orientation can be varied (see Figure 25) Walking past each other by starting at different points on a figure of eight. Walking round each other in a small semi-circle.
o	'Piggy in the middle' The odd one out, e.g. 2 to have something in common such as costume, or 2 males and 1 female. Being pulled in 2 directions The eternal triangle Meeting, parting, 'three's a crowd'.	Line, triangle, circle Overlap (see Figure 26) (see Figure 27 for examples of formations)	Passing through Splitting Linking Constant changes in direction are effective, and in numerical grouping, e.g. 2 + 1, 3 all together. Trios co-existing
uartet	'We are a group' 3 surrounding one 3 against one 3 protecting or comforting one	Square, regular formation, 2 lines	3 + 1; 1 + 1 + 1 + 1; 4 together; 2 + 2; 2 + 1 + 1 A particularly effective transition is moving from two pairs to become a group of four, and vice versa. Exploitation of the symmetry of the foursome.
uintet	'We are a group' Us and them Us and the one left out Us and our leader	Lines × 2 Circle Half Circle	2 + 3; 2 + 2 + 1; 2 + 1 + 1 + 1; 4 + 1; 5 together; 1 + 1 + 1 + 1 + 1 Surrounding Leading Following Going through the gaps Quintet groups co-existing (see Figure 28)

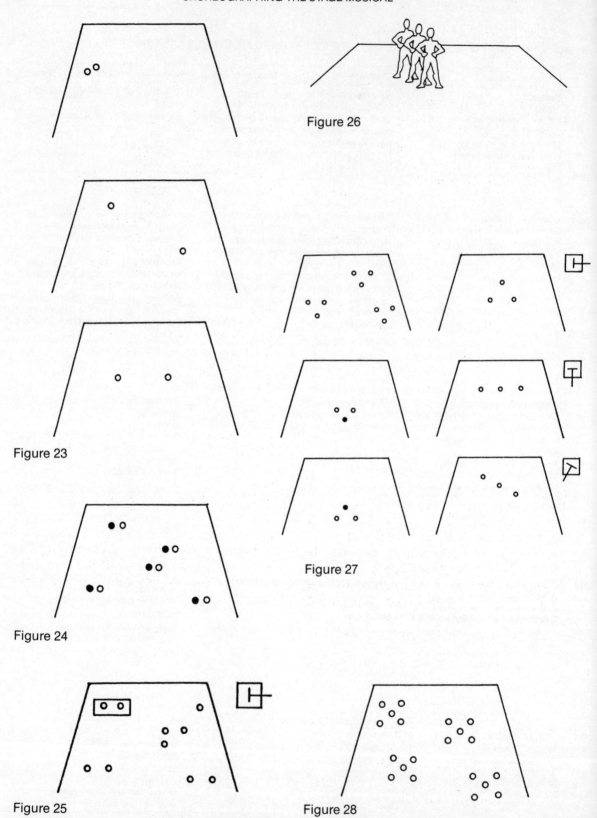

Figure 26

Figure 23

Figure 24

Figure 25

Figure 27

Figure 28

Irregular Formations and Achieving Organised Chaos

Sometimes regular formations are inapprop-riate to the choreography of a musical: a mill-ing crowd, the preoccupation of people with their busy lives, the varied activity of market or village are all best conveyed by a more random grouping, even though it is vital to keep some element of choreographic order. A subtle but important distinction must be made between the total confusion that would result if all such crowd scenes were entirely improvised and the 'ordered chaos' that is created by the choreographer, albeit using improvisation as a means to this end. There will often be a difficult stage in rehearsal when the choreographer appears to be achieving neither spontaneity nor order, but a state of untidyness that is simply irritating; this is when a knowledge of some simple but effective devices will be par-ticularly useful and we outline some of these below, as suggestions for avoiding the state of panic that can so easily creep into the inexpe-rienced choreographer's work at such times.

Crossing

Busy activity can be suggested by people crossing in front of each other, exiting and then perhaps re-entering soon after at another part of the stage. The length of the floor pat-terns and the speed and rhythm with which performers travel along them can also be varied. The notation of such floor patterns may be very intricate but it is vital, however, that such crossings should be actually choreo-graphed rather than improvised in order that an optimum level of variety be achieved.

Variety of Grouping and Activity

When choreographing a milling crowd in such situations as village scenes, dancers in solos, duos or trios may move in amongst static groups of various sizes. Other individuals may simply be going about their tasks, walking, gesturing, laughing or running. Thus a hive of activity can be created by using a whole variety or movements and groupings. Such an app-roach would also be appropriate in choreo-graphing a disco, a party, a celebration and even a riot. The disco dance or hop, like those in *West Side Story* and *Grease* for example, could entail the simultaneous events of men chatting up girls in doorways (using exaggera-ted gesture), circles of people clapping, others holding handbags, trios doing the pogo, men chasing women, drunks crawling on the floor (in unison and with a rhythmic structure of course!), and five sets of double duo work dancing rock 'n' roll. Within this apparent 'chaos' therefore, sections of arranged spatial ordering and groupings can be used to pro-vide clarity and appeal which improvised chaos often lacks.

Hysteria

Panic and more extreme chaos can be achieved by introducing the added element of charac-ters bumping into each other rather than skil-fully crossing. When the hysterical group is to be stationary, ensure that it is totally disparate by choreographing as much variety in terms of width of gap, level, direction and place of focus as possible. To begin with this may be achieved by allowing performers to take up random positions on stage, but will almost certainly need 'polishing' to avoid repetition.

7. Dealing with the Co-Existence of Groups

Figure 1

When more than one group is present on stage at any one time the harmonious balance that ensures that one group complements another requires the artistry of a sensitive eye. A number of points can contribute to effective choreography in this situation:

a) Allow Sufficient Room to Accommodate All Groups

Firstly, do not overcrowd but see that there is sufficient space both practically and aesthetically to accommodate the different groups. For example, in Figure 1, the juxtaposition of

these two different groups does not really 'work' because both designs require a good deal of surrounding empty space to be fully effective. There are also too many groups, so that the two designs appear over-intricate and over-repeated and the eye is unable to determine where to settle. For similar reasons, the choreography of Figure 2 is unsatisfactory; the stage is too full and demands too much attention and concentration from the spectator. This may be contrasted with the comfortable co-existence achieved in Figure 3.

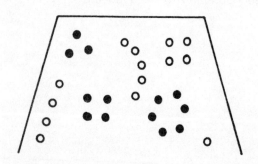

Figure 2

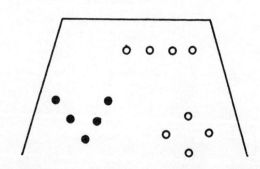

Figure 3

b) Co-existence Will Affect Each Group Present

The semi-circular formation may lose some of its inherent roundness and softness if it is placed next to a sharp angled triangle, as shown in Figure 4. Likewise, Figure 5 illustrates

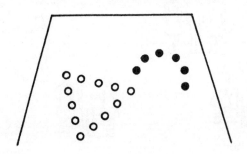

Figure 4

how the surrounding group on a rostrum level has a softening effect on the enclosed wedge. On the other hand, this so-called 'interference' can be used by the choreographer to produce particular merging effects.

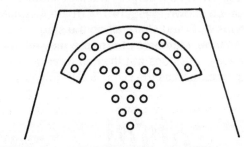

Figure 5

c) Too similar groups can be hard to distinguish from one another. If co-existing groups already share some aspects, their juxtaposition will often seem pleasing and complementary. In Figure 6 for example, the two groups share the same distance between

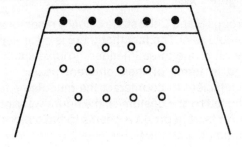

Figure 6

members. If, however, the two groups have too much in common, they may seem to merge into one; this is beginning to happen in Figure 7 where the line and the block are not seen as two distinct formations; instead,

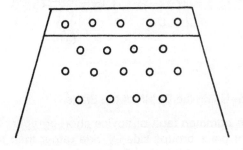

Figure 7

the line appears to be simply an extension of the block despite its added height from the rostrum. A solution would have been to vary the distance between members of the two

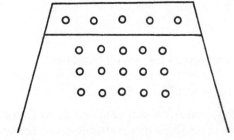

Figure 8

groups as shown in Figure 8. In Figure 9a again the group differences are insufficiently marked and demand the greater variation of Figure 9b.

Figure 9a

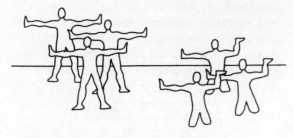

Figure 9b

d) Using the Depth of the Stage

A common fault of novice choreographers is to place groups side by side rather than forward and back (see Figure 10) and thus create no sense of depth and lead to focusing problems.

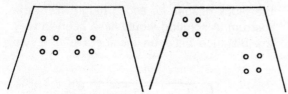

Figure 10

e) Distinguish between Intentional, Pre-planned and Clear Cross-groupings and Groups which Lack Sufficient Uniformity

Intentional cross-grouping occurs when members of the same group sharing some common feature, such as body design or costume, are spatially separate or even share an area of the stage with members of another group or groups. An example of this is shown in Figure 11 where members of each group can be identified as having the same body design. They do

Figure 11

not stand together, however. A similarly effective piece of cross-grouping is shown in Fig. 12 where the effect is achieved by a simple difference in costume.

Figure 12

Sometimes, however, cross-referencing is not the effect that the choreographer is seeking. He may wish figures standing together to appear as a unified group, but because they lack sufficient uniformity, they may seem to have more in common with figures standing elsewhere on the stage. Take for example the situation shown in Figure 13a where the three groups A, B and C are all on the stage at the same time. Members of group A may all hold the same positions but they all wear different costumes, and as the same is also true of

Figure 13a

groups B and C the stage actually resembles a jumble sale! The fact that there is clear separation of the three intended groups, spatially and in terms of their different positions, is insufficient to counteract the muddled effect caused by the costumes: the figure wearing a short skirt in group A seems to have more in common with the figure wearing the same in group B, than with members of her own group even though she shares their position. Now look at the same design in 13b where there is no 'interference' from costume. Other problems in relation to cross referencing are often the result of inadequate polishing at rehearsal where small deviations in level, focus or direction are allowed to creep in.

Figure 13b

f) Give the Spectator Guidance as to Where to Look and When

Co-existing groups can so often cause frustrating problems of visual competition. It may be impossible to decide where to look first. A spectator confronted by three groups may, for example, be worried that she may miss some vital part of the action in one group if she looks at another. It is therefore essential that the choreographer builds in clues as to where the audience should focus its attention. This is not the same as saying that the choreographer should ensure that the audience sees every tiny movement of every performer; indeed, in any temporal medium some details and subtleties will be missed by any one spectator. We are simply advocating that the audience should be made to feel comfortable in its viewing and not pressured by the feeling that 'understanding' the dance depends on a race against time. In the list which follows we outline some of the means by which a choreographer can ensure that the audience has clear guidelines for attention:

Attention-attracting devices

1. Motion: movement attracts the eye more than stillness; a figure may become conspicuous the moment it starts to move.

2. Colour: some colours are immediately more noticeable on account of their shorter wavelengths: examples include red and blue.

3. Position on stage; weak and strong areas have already been defined; people facing downstage are generally more conspicuous than those facing upstage.

4. Speech: visual attention is inevitably drawn towards any performer who speaks and thus a singing group is likely to attract more attention than a silent one.

5. Energy change: if one group begins to move with more staccato or rapid movement or if there is a change in spatial relationship within the group the audience's attention will be re-focused.

6. Gaze: directional pointers caused by the dancer looking in a particular direction can be called 'visual lines': the audience's attention will follow the visual lines of the performers; this has both advantages and dangers: the attention of an audience will be drawn towards any group being watched by the rest of the cast but also towards any performer with a different facial expression from the others.

7. Body facing: dancers may actually turn or even point towards a group who are intended to be the focus of attention.

8. Spatial isolation: Figures 14a & b illustrate this point.

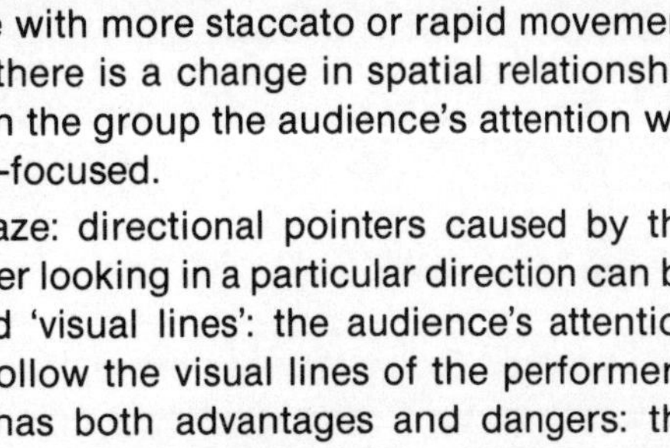

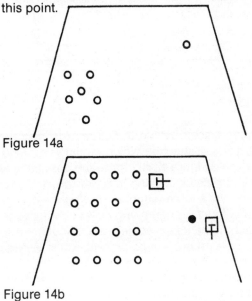

Figure 14a

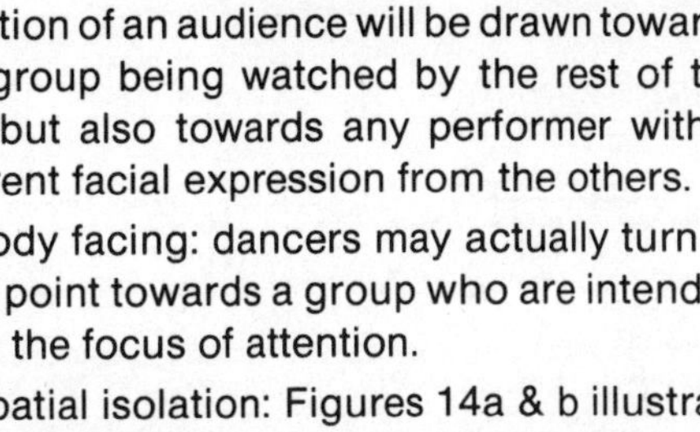

Figure 14b

9. Light: Obviously dancers in a brightly lit area will attract more attention than those in darker areas of the stage.

Clearly, the choreographer must ensure that these various devices do not cancel each other out.There are also a number of other simple ways in which visual competition may be avoided and these mainly concern aspects of

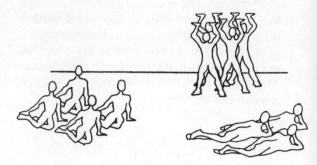

Figure 17

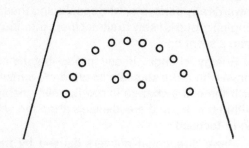

Figure 15

positioning. Figure 15, for example, shows how one group 'frames' another simply by

Figure 18

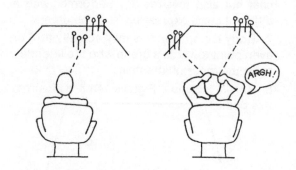

Figure 16

being placed behind it. Figure 16 shows the sort of 'split attention' which should be avoided, whereas Figure 17 illustrates the possibility of the spectator looking over or beyond one group to another. Figures 18-23 give suggestions for choreographing co-existing groups; each figure keeps some features common to all co-existing groups present whilst varying others such as level, direction, number in a group, distance between group members, formation and costume.

Figure 19

Figure 20

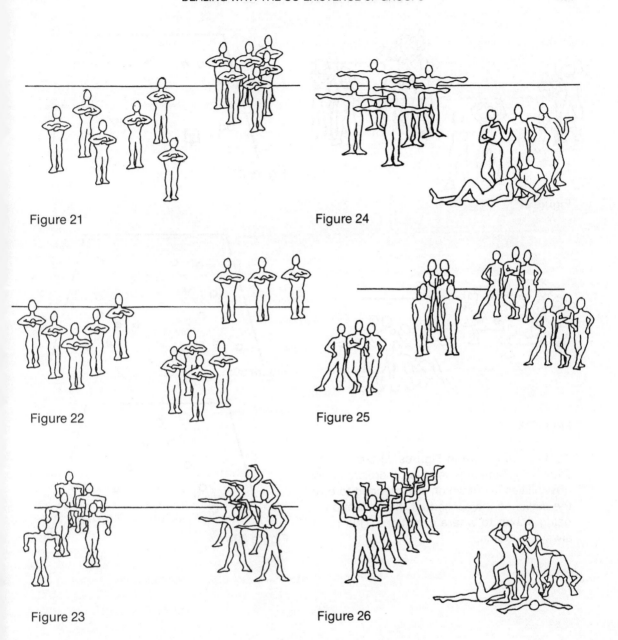

Figure 21

Figure 24

Figure 22

Figure 25

Figure 23

Figure 26

The art of juxtaposing different groups may also involve the use of clash, direct opposites and contradictions. Formal groups, for example, gain visual interest when set against more naturalistic groupings (see Figures 24, 25, 26, 27 and 28) and similar experiments may be made with colour, mood, sex and costume shape. Perhaps the most powerful device is the juxtaposition of the soloist with the chorus.

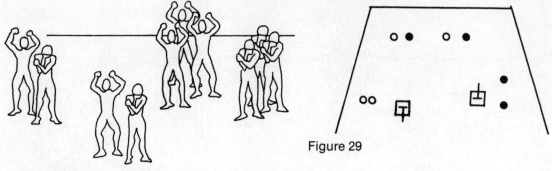

Figure 27

Figure 29

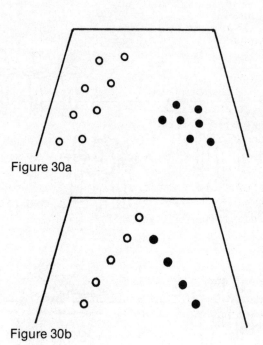

Figure 30a

Figure 28

As we have shown in Figures 29-30b, which show male/female ensembles, there are many possibilities, all of which are intended to give the audience the sense that their attention is being drawn to where it matters. This must always be our aim.

Figure 30b

8. Transition Techniques

If we look at any design for a long while, the initial interest is bound to fade and the eye seeks some change, conversely, abrupt changes in visual impact lead to a sense of bewilderment. The choreographer has to take both these factors into account in order to achieve that balance which will keep the spectator's attention. Choreographers and dancers experience similar anxieties about affecting transitions from one position to another: the type of problem they face is illustrated in Figure 1 where the choreographer must decide how to move the five dancers out of grouping A to B and then C. Remember that it is important to think of 'melting' or 'dissolving' into the next formation rather than 'shifting' or 'exchanging'. In other words avoid contrived and over obvious manoeuvres.

Transition should be smooth and polished, movement motivated by preceding events. The audience should be able to see relationship between one event and the next. We have illustrated this in Figure 2 where the 'C's move to the 'B's who in turn begin to approach the 'A's who react by moving as well. In this example the transitions are motivated by the approach of other dancers, the ripple effect being achieved through the transference of energy and momentum. Remember the importance of not pausing at the moment of contact here, otherwise the continuity of the movement may well be lost. This may require some sensitive rehearsal. Other transitions may not benefit from such 'movement motivation' and in such cases it is often appropriate to run or walk to the new formation by the simplest possible route, avoiding elaborate floor patterns,

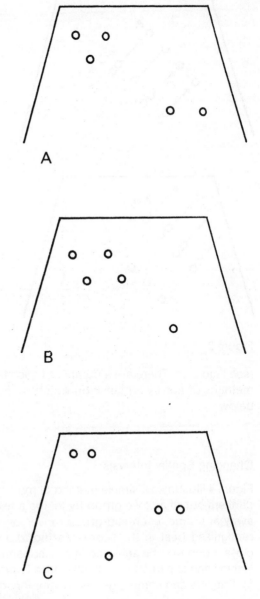

Figure 1

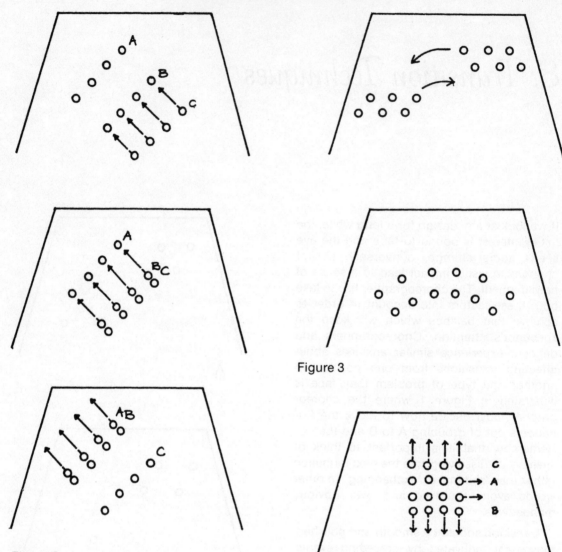

Figure 2

Figure 3

Figure 4

(see Figure 3). There are a number of specific methods of achieving tansition which we list below:

Changing Spatial Intervals

Figure 4 illustrates a simple method of moving dancers out of a close group by taking a few away at a time, each sub-group moves on a recognised beat in the score. Moving *into* a close group may be achieved in similar canon fashion and is particularly effective (see Figure 5). Dancers can come together by running, or

by a series of small jumps in ripple canon which will slowly reduce the amount of space occupied by the group, all the more pleasing if there is a contrast between the original formation and the shape of the group at the completion of the transition. In Figure 6, for example, a group making abstract gestures, changes to become a naturalistic close group for a few bars before returning to its original formation and movement vocabulary. It is sometimes alarming to a choreographer if the planned transitions leave a large gap on the stage. The

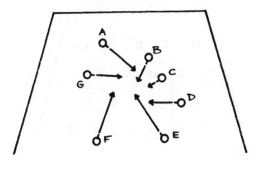

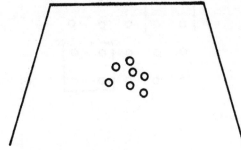

Figure 5

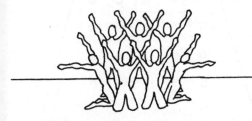

Figure 6

Inherent or Hidden Structures

Figures 8-13 show some of the structures which may be concealed within an already existing grouping and which may be used as the next formation; squares, triangles and other interesting shapes exist within larger shapes and may be revealed in a transition. It is also possible for a square within an oblong, for example to move in a different way from the rest of the group, thus revealing the new shape. Figure 14 shows a line placed beside a triangle. After a while, a member of the line suddenly joins in with the movements of the triangle thus entirely changing the structure of the two groups.

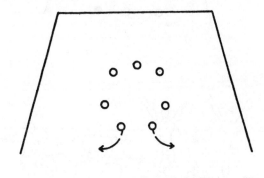

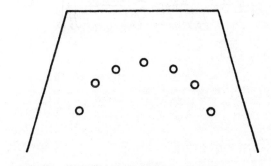

Figure 8

solution, as indicated in Figure 7, is for another group to flow into the space. Whatever the choreographer decides, the important thing is for transitions to be carried out without loss of energy momentum.

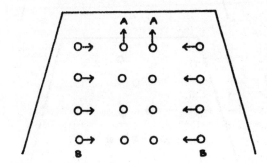

Figure 7

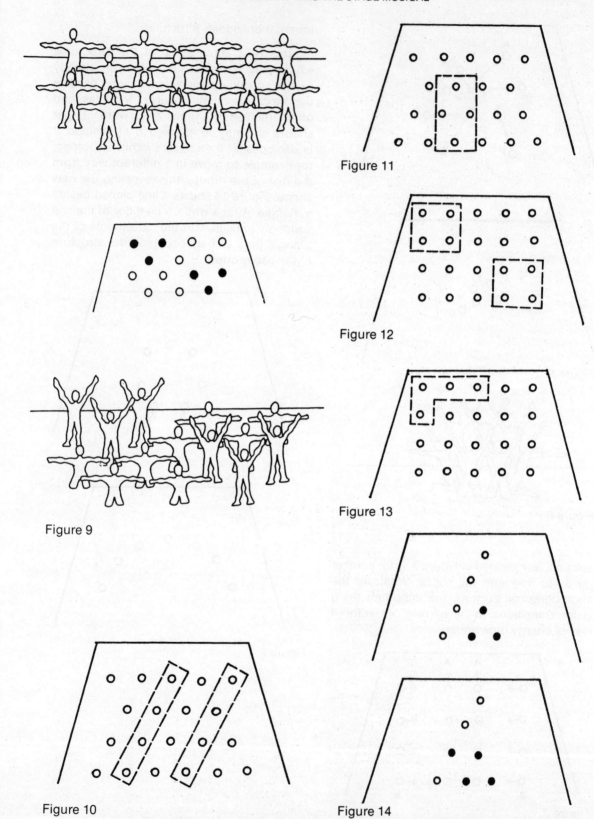

Figure 11

Figure 12

Figure 13

Figure 9

Figure 10

Figure 14

Entrances and Exits

It is sometimes best for a transition to be achieved by characters leaving and entering the stage; this may be brought about by reducing or increasing the numbers to achieve a spatial change. In Figure 15 four people perform a short movement sequence during which, at intervals perhaps of about eight bars of music, a new character runs on to the stage and picks up the movement being performed at that moment. This happens four times and eventually eight people are dancing in unison. This whole process could be carried out in reverse so that the arrival of a newcomer makes the group change their movement to

During a dance, certain performers may suddenly leave, perhaps in different numbers. From a group of eight, for example, the choreographer may subtract one, three together, then a couple and then one again so that a solo performer is left. Such a canon effect may lead to a fall of energy level if the dancers are not re-introduced, and this may have to be compensated for by an increase in the volume of music or an energy change in the remaining soloist. At the climax of an exit canon sequence, the soloist may attempt to fill far more of the stage with vigorous movement as if liberated.

Entrances and exits may be made particularly effective if there is a marked contrast in the design and energy level of different groups;

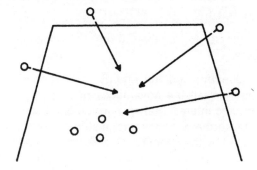

Figure 15

copy that introduced. Figure 16 shows how whole dance sequences can be built around such joining in and juxtaposing.

1. Group A enter, dance sequence A and exit.
2. Group B enter, dance sequence B and exit.
3. Group C enter, dance sequence C and exit.
4. Group A enter using motifs from B and C's routines.
5. Group A is joined by group B and together they dance B's sequence.
6. Group C enter and dance certain movements from sequence A, B, and C.
7 and 8. Group C is joined by groups A and B. All three groups then dance in unison and perform movements from all three routines. The three groups finish by 'co-existing' but performing their own original sequence once. The finishing position is a shared movement performed in unison and taken from group B's sequence.

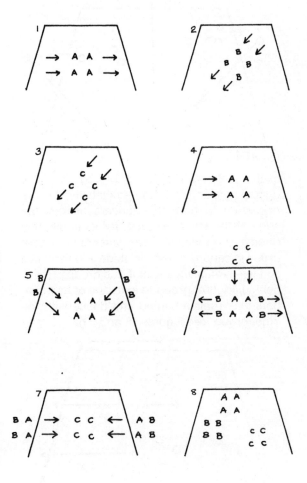

Figure 16

for example, in Figure 17 two clumps using tiny shuffling steps with no arm movements move onto the stage, cross and then exit; as they are about to disappear four other dancers enter from various directions with high, speedy, peripheral jumps like exploding fireworks and then move to the front of the stage. Similarly

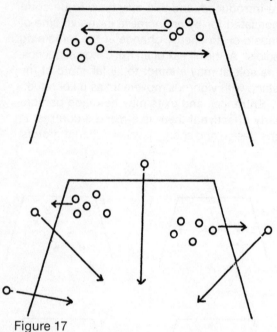

Figure 17

exciting effects may be achieved by introducing an element of unpredictability; it is not necessary to have the dancers nearest the edge of the stage exit first, for example. It is often a good idea to have dancers who have exited in canon, to rush on stage in unison in a sudden re-appearance; or if one group crosses behind another group to exit, one of its members may remain behind and dance with the other group (see Figures 18 and 19).

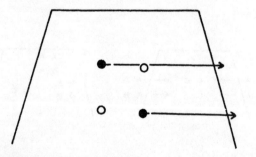

Figure 18

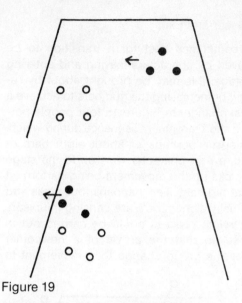

Figure 19

Points to Remember about Entrances and Exits

1. Queuing and the energy loss of the late entrance: all the advantages of surprise and renewed interest that we have outlined are lost if performers arrive late. Lateness may be caused by the opening of doors onto the set or by the fact that an entrance is too narrow so that a queue forms. Obstacles such as steps or lighting stands may have to be navigated in the dark and exits may be made difficult by very congested wing space. There are even some stages where performers have to duck suddenly to avoid low slung girders the moment they are off stage and this can cause even greater problems in reverse! It is therfore vital for the choreographer to explore all the entrances and exits and to adapt the movements of the cast accordingly. One solution for difficult exits is for dancers to peel off in canon (see Figure 20) and particular care must be

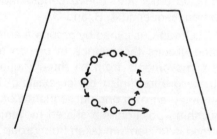

Figure 20

taken in planning sequences in which vigorous movement begins off stage leading to an explosive entry.

2. Entrances must be prepared for, so that the audience is drawn to look towards the incoming character; interesting activity going on elsewhere will distract from the desired effect. When there is to be a succession of entrances it is important to have a time overlap so that momentum and energy are not lost and it is essential not to leave the stage bare in the middle of a dance.

3. The effect of an entrance and exit depends substantially on the place where it is made; the four corners of a stage are visually strong and easily noticeable places, whereas centre side entrances and exits may easily go undetected. Downstage exits will convey a sense of urgency and speed and, by contrast, the upstage exit is appropriate for long, slow, dignified and processional effects. Some choreographers claim that because we read from left to right an entrance from stage right is both more noticeable and capable of achieving an illusion of great speed, as it is the usual way in which we watch activity; it is certainly the case that there is a tradition in pantomime for good characters to enter from the left and wicked characters from the right.

Transitions by Crossing Through the Gap

Very appealing visual effects may be achieved by dancers crossing in front or behind each other. There are various ways of executing such crossings:

1. Passing through - Figures 21 and 22.

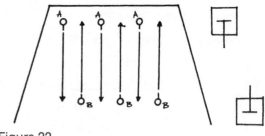

Figure 22

2. Passing in front, at the back or by the side - Figures 23, 24a and b.

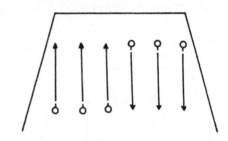

Figure 23

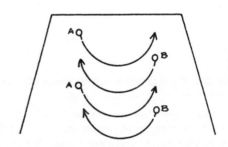

Figure 24a

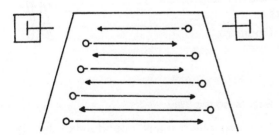

Figure 21

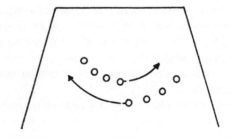

Figure 24b

3. Crossing over - Figure 25.

4. Passing in between - Figure 26.

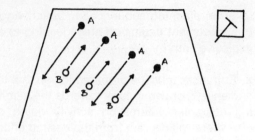

Figure 27a

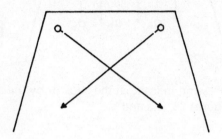

Figure 25

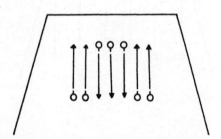

Figure 26

Variations in Speed, Direction and Movement Vocabulary

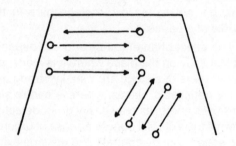

Figure 27b

These can emphasise the distinctions between the 'crossers' and those crossing; it is not necessary to assume that crossing has to take place with groups facing each other: in Figure 27a, for example, dancers are crossing but the B group is walking backwards. During a crossing, two groups may change the direction in which they are facing and two separate groups of direction crossing can be performed simultaneously as in Figure 27b. Crossers and those crossing may each have their own movement sequence: in Figure 22 the 'A's could cross through the 'B's with a low and symmetrical movement whilst the 'B's cross with high movements and decorative, asymmetrical arm movements.

Remarkable effects can be gained by choreographing crossings in very slow motion as if the dancers are under hypnosis, or very fast, like speeding traffic. A refinement of these

ideas is for a very fast group to cross through a very slow group or, ideally, for a single performer to cross at a totally different speed from a group as if passing through a rushing crowd. The danger and risk of such events is often exhilarating: an example of this is shown in Figure 28 where couples with ballroom holds are moving past each other through very small gaps. This would be appropriate for the finale of Olklahoma or the ballroom scene in Call Me Madam.

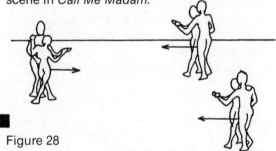

Figure 28

Events on the Way

Crossing offers many opportunities for the unpredictable happening; spectators tend to assume that a crossing will simply continue to the point of completion but one of the following events may occur on the way:

1. Dancers stop at random or even double back (Figure 29);

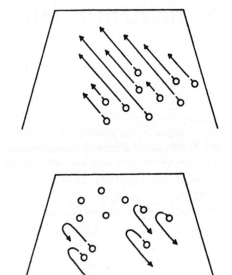

Figure 29

2. One member of a group may change direction or even pass through moving backwards;
3. Groups may stop and freeze and another group start to move.

Transitions from Song to Dance, Dance to Dialogue and Vice-Versa

The sudden transition from one dramatic medium to another should appear perfectly natural although there may be times when its shock impact is what the director is seeking. It is of course a highly *unnatural* piece of behaviour for anyone to break from dialogue into song or dance, and although this is easily accepted as a convention of the Musical the transitions must be handled with skill. This is particularly the case where the audience must switch from the comparative reality of recognisable every-day speech in the form of dialogue to the obvious fantasy world created by dance. Changes of medium must be smooth and rapid, any hesitation soon reveals the gaps and the momentum is lost. So often there are clumsy transitions from naturalistic, informal grouping to the very obvious design of a set dance formation. Matters are made worse if dancers arrive in position too early and appear to be waiting for the music to begin. Equally clumsy transititons occur when the use of microphones is involved and performers have to move out of a conversation or dance number to pick up or sing into a microphone. Audiences are very sensitive to the worried glances of the cast looking round to see if every one is ready for a number to begin. All such problems can be avoided by careful planning and rehearsal: in a transition it is wise not to stop everything at once so (for example, when there is a transition to be made from dialogue to dance) the characters should keep talking and moving until the music begins - silence only draws attention to the change. The cast should be rehearsed in walking to a singing position (whether to a microphone or not) by the shortest possible route and as a perfectly acceptable convention of the piece.

The choreographer can even contribute to the most elaborate transitions in the theatre: complete changes of scenery, by having dancers in front of the curtain or set change; this is known as a crossover.

9. Using Music and Structuring Time

If a decision has been taken to use dance or gesture in a certain number, it is then important to consider exactly how music and movement should inter-relate. Just as it is necessary to consider how much to imitate the lyrics, it is equally vital to consider how much to imitate the music. Should the dance echo, parallel or highlight the metre, rhythms, use of leitmotif, accents, tempos, crescendos, counterpoint, phrasing, etc. in the music? In order to answer this, when choreographing consider the requirements of each particular number in terms of the role of the music at that particular moment in the musical. Decide whether music is intended to be the dominant medium at the time or dance. In other words whether dance is there to add colour and support to the music or vice versa. Consider whether the music is there to heighten energy, to soothe, to arouse sympathy or to excite. Decide when dance could help to achieve any of these ends.

On occasions close paralleling of the music would be unsuccessful. In musical accompaniment of great complexity, dance could not hope to mark the many changes of time signature - 3/8 - 5/16 - 8/9. If dance was attempted here, it would be likely to destroy the metric subtleties in the music. Sometimes, however, dance may be chosen to go directly against the music. If, for example, the music is suggesting the 'baddie' and therefore is slow, pounding and of ominous tones, the 'goodies' may choose to dance with a panicky fast tempoed staccato reaction. It can indeed be delightful to use choreography which is a direct contrast to the music, to choreograph nonmetric dance with metric music, for example, or to use nonmetric music for metric dance, or to employ extremes in tempos, differences in numbers of accents in a phrase, etc. in the two art forms. If this is the choreographer's choice, he should realise that this does not give him permission to be blissfully oblivious of the music and its structure. As Schuller (*Dance Perspectives* No. 16, p. 38) points out -

> If the choreographer consistently ignores the metric and phrasing shapes of the music . . . it is like reading a book in which the printer has put all the commas and periods in the middle of sentences and clauses.

With particular dances where style is important, for example, ballroom dances or a social dance such as the charleston, the phrasing of the music plays a major part in conveying that style and, therefore, the choreographic phrasing must be complementary and supportive to that of the music. In other words, make sure that the choreography is not in a different style to that of the music. With certain differences in phrasing the spectator is likely to receive highly conflicting messages.

Find out how many musicians will be playing each dance number. If there are far more instruments playing than dancers dancing at any one time, the music may seem 'too big' for the dance. In other words, the dance may seem little more than an annoying distraction, similar to the effect of a small fly buzzing around on a huge expanse of wall. The matching of solo instruments to a solo dance can often produce a state of sympathetic beauty.

Structuring Time

1. Phrasing and Pausing

The use of the pause is relatively well developed and understood in most art forms. Both music and written and spoken language have standard forms of notation for indicating a subtle variety of pauses. In our view, the pause is equally important in dance, but it seems to have been unreasonably neglected and its use by the choreographer often seems to be much less well thought out. Although dance has more freedom in terms of choices of positioning and duration of the pauses and fewer rules than is the case in other art forms, it is often used unimaginatively or carelessly, whereas careful attention to pauses can often provide a dance with a logical continuity of movement, a feeling of pace, design and momentum.

Novice choreographers tend to create phrases which are too short and of equal length. This often means that the choreography comprises a succession of 'run run pose' 'run run pose' movements. This is illustrated with the concept of the spectator's 'tension balloon' in Figure 1. This demonstrates that because the phrases are too short, insufficient energy has been built up before the pause, consequently the balloon deflates during each pause, resulting in a drop in energy level and a decrease in interest and excitement for the spectator.

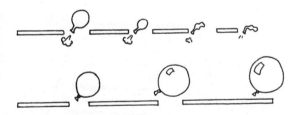

Figure 1

A long phrase of movement on the other hand will tend to gather momentum and energy which will be carried over into the pause and thus inflate the spectator's balloon. Pay close attention, therefore, to the position and duration of each pause. Unnecessary lengthening of the pause itself, just as over-frequent pausing, can have a destructive effect on the pace and tension of the piece. In other words, an over-long break in the flow of

movement may well lead to a break in the flow of thought for the spectator, the gap allowing the spectator's mind to wander to something other than the dance. In addition, consider how the pause is to come about. It can happen suddenly or gradually. Movement can be immediately resumed or very gradually. Each has a different effect. With a song, the choreographer may parallel the phrasing of the lyrics, the inflexions and multistresses of the polysyllabic words in the dance. Using the punctuation from lyrics in this way can lead to a sensitively phrased dance.

2. The Spatial and Temporal Void

It is important to recognise the power of both silence and stillness. Each can be used to highlight or emphasise. Various examples of uses and effects of pausing and freezing are outlined below:

(i) *The Pause.* A pause can be used to evoke suspense, tension or surprise, just as can the carefully positioned moment of silence in a written sentence:
'He went, and he looked, and there it was —— a mouse!'
(long pause)
Suspense in a dance can be gained, therefore, from a long pause preceding a final sudden impactive movement. A pause can draw attention to the movement immediately preceding it. The pause in this case has a similar role to the exclamation mark at the end of a written sentence. The feeling and essence of the previous movement can be carried over into the stillness. A long pause at the end of a movement phrase may give a sense of importance to that phrase or a feeling of finality.

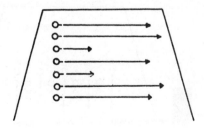

Figure 2

(ii) *The Freeze.* This idea can have great dramatic impact when used in a choreography.

a) Members of a group suddenly stop in the middle of a movement phrase whilst the other members keep moving (Figure 2).

b) One figure remains constantly still as people enter, walk past him and exit (Figure 3).

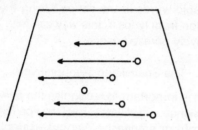

Figure 3

(iii) *Group Exchange of Motion and Stillness.*

a) Group B dance, Group A act as a human backcloth and freeze in one of the positions that Group B will perform at some time during their dance (possibly the main motif of the piece). At the moment Group B reach this chosen position, the two groups are seen to be connected. Groups A and B may then exchange roles, Group B becoming the static group, group A dancing.

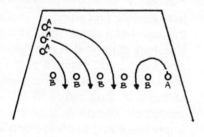

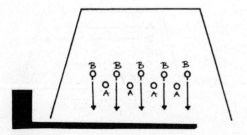

Figure 4

b) Group A run through Group B who are still. Group A then themselves freeze, and immediately Group B start to move and run through the stationary Group A (see Figure 4).

(iv) *Flock of Birds.* Members of a group run on stage, one after another in ripple canon. Each of them freeze in turn and hold their position as the others join them. The effect is one resemblant of a flock of birds gradually descending from the sky (Figure 5).

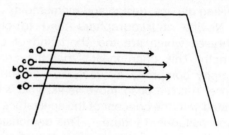

Figure 5

(v) *Collecting the 'Freezers'.* Members of Group B freeze. Group A start to move. As they pass the Bs, the Bs are motivated into movement and start walking with the As (Figure 6).

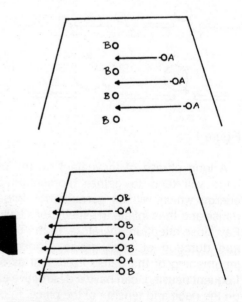

Figure 6

(vi) *A Succession of Poses.* A chorus may perform one naturalistic pose, freeze for a time, then change into another pose. Whenever adopting this 'pose freeze pose' idea, exaggerate the transition from one pose to another. Make it a large, immediately noticeable movement before settling back into stillness again.

(vii) *Odd One Out.* The group start to dance in unison. Suddenly one dancer freezes in one of the movements as if capturing an image in a still photograph whilst the other members of the group continue the sequence. A freeze like this soon gathers interest. Is she going to move again, and if so, when? (Figure 7)

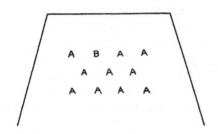

Figure 7

Rhythm for Emotional Expression

Many emotions have associative rhythms. Frustration and irritation, for example, are often associated with a regular tapping foot; anger with the staccato rhythm; panic and fear with irregular accents and frequent irregular pauses, and mounting anxiety with a cumulative rhythm - 1, 1 2, 1 2 3, 1 2 3 4, etc. With more calm emotions, phrases tend to be longer, more even and regular. Think of the comfort of rocking, for example.

Irregular Accenting

Often the constant repetition of a simple rhythm with regular accents is very attractive. It can provide a feeling of balance, stability and security. At other times, however, it is appropriate to use irregular accented patterns and unexpected breaks in continuity. In a 7/4 time signature, for example, the rhythm can be organised in such a way that the grouping of the 7 beats is not always the same:

```
    4   &   3   /   3   &   4   /        7      /
    1 2 3 4 5 6 7   1 2 3 4 5 6 7   1 2 3 4 5 6 7
            7   /       2, 2, 3,   /   2, 3, 2
    1 2 3 4 5 6 7   1 2 3 4 5 6 7   1 2 3 4 5 6 7
```

In the example below, the line of dancers run on the spot and on the notes marked with accents they lift and drop their arms:

4/4   1 2 3 4 / 1 2 3 4 / 1 2 3 4 / 1 2 3 4 /

Or two groups may dance three bars of 5/4 using the same movements but accenting each phrase at different places:

Group A   1 2 3 4 5/ 1 2 3 4 5/ 1 2 3 4 5/
- accenting every 3rd beat

Group B   1 2 3 4 5/ 1 2 3 4 5/ 1 2 3 4 5/
- accenting every 5th beat.

This idea would also be effective if both groups used different movements and different accents whilst sharing the pulse, tempo and time signature.

Syncopation

Sycopation means accenting the usually *un*-accented beats, omitting some of the down beats or strong beats, and accenting some of the up or weak beats. For example:

4/4   1 2 3 - / 1 & 2 - 4 / 1 2 & 3 4 /
- & 2 - 3 - 4 /.

(the dash in this example indicates a held movement).

Syncopation is a particular method of rhythmic emphasis used in both music and dance but not used in written or spoken language due to the adverse effects it would have on the understanding of the meaning of the sentence! An example of a syncopated sentence would be:

'He went, up the, hill and - sat down looking at, the view, in front of - him'.

It can be particularly exciting rhythmically when two groups are on stage, for one group

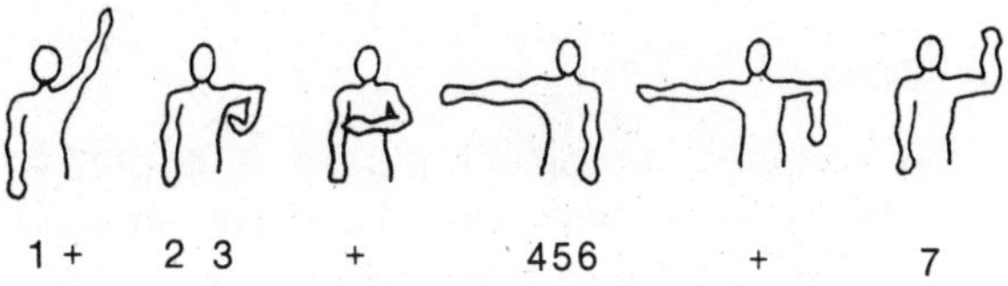

1 +   2 3   +   456   +   7

Figure 8

to use regular accents and stress the pulse whilst the other group syncopates. A succession of gestures is often very attractive if performed with syncopated phrasing (see Figure 8) or try using naturalistic gestures or mannerisms. People waiting in a queue, as for example in 'The Great Feminine Struggle' (*Mothers and Daughters*) and 'Food Glorious Food' (*Oliver*) may dance a succession of syncopated gestures including foot tapping, looking at a watch, scratching the head, straightening a leg, whilst an office scene, such as part of the song 'There Must Be Something Better Than This' (*Sweet Charity*) and scenes from *How to Succeed in Business Without Really Trying* may include syncopated sequences of typing, throwing paper in a bin, drinking coffee, and throwing up the hands with frustration. Syncopated foot patterns are delightful for small groups where the feet are easily visible to the spectator. Or a solo dancer may 'play' his body in two parts. His lower body may pause or keep pulse whilst the upper body moves to a syncopated rhythm.

Tempo

Most musicals operate at a fast speed. Fast movements can generate energy and excitement. To achieve a sense of speed, remember that the smaller the confines of space, the faster the motion will seem. Moreover, if fast motion is juxtaposed to stillness or slow motion, it will seem even faster. Extremes of tempo in movement, the very fast vibration or jitter or the very slow walk or gesture can be very impactive and eye catching. So can acceleration or deceleration over a long period. These both usually benefit from a substantial pause at the end of the phrase. A change of speed with a change of activity, for example, a fast run ending in a slow fall recovering into a fast turn attracts interest by being unpredictable.

Canon

A canoned movement phrase is a phrase where dancers start to move one after another, usually in quick succession. Canon can be abysmally predictable and as a result the spec-

tator quickly loses interest in the repetition of the movement pattern. To avoid predictability, it is possible to vary the tempo or rhythm of a canoned phrase, or the performers can start to dance at irregular intervals:

Dancer's Number - 1 2   3   4 5 6
Phrase   1 2 3 & 4 5 6 7 & 8

In repeating the movement, members of a group may vary the level, direction or size of the movement when it comes to their turn. If the 'tension balloon' is to stay inflated in a canoned phrase, it is important to gain momentum during the repeats. This can be achieved by accelerating slightly and thus introducing a sense of an approaching climax. Pausing after each person moves, prior to the start of the next person will only create a disjointed fragmented impression. One way to ensure that there is no tension loss is to use 'ripple canon'. This is when one performer starts to move *during* not after, the previous person has finished their movement or movement sequence. This way each individual's movement becomes part of the whole canoned spatial design and temporal phrase. If, however, movements are overlapped too much in ripple canon it may be misinterpreted as 'untogether' unison. Ripple canon can be a particularly useful device to camouflage poor transitions, sitting down to standing up for example. A full stop at the end of a canoned phrase, however, is often appropriate. It is important not to throw away the final impression of the end of the canoned phrase by moving too quickly into the next phrase. Aim for a good balance of unison and canon work in a dance. Too much of one for too long becomes monotonous. Also consider how long to repeat the movement in a canoned phrase. However 'rippled' or overlapping each movement is, if it is carried on for too long, some of the last repeats will seem redundant.

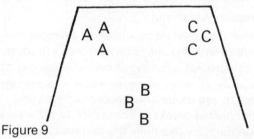

Figure 9

Several different ways of canoning are set out below. Each example is using a set sequence comprising six movements:

1. Canon with Clear Spatial Blocking (see Figure 9). As move on count 1, Bs on count 2, Cs on count 3.

2. Canon with more Random Grouping (see Figure 10a, b, c, d). As move on count 1, Bs on count 2, Cs on count 3, Ds on count 4, etc.

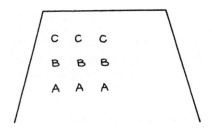

Figure 10a

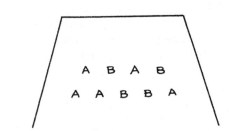

Figure 10b

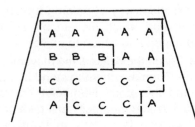

Figure 10c

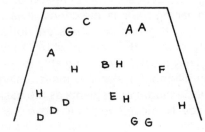

Figure 10d

3. Canon with Level Variation (Figure 11)

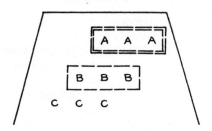

Figure 11

4. Echoing or Dialogue Canon (see Figure 12a and b). The As begin on count 1, the Bs on count 3. The As hold a finishing position after the sixth movement and wait until the Bs catch up. When the Bs reach the sixth position they freeze, and the As start again. The Bs join in on the As' third movement as before. The pattern recommences. Alternatively, the As could perform the whole sequence and hold whilst the Bs perform it, rather than coming in during the As' performance.

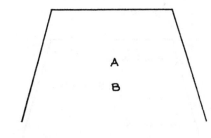

Figure 12a

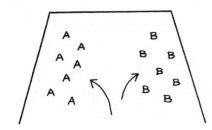

Figure 12b

5. Rotation Canon. There are six dancers performing the six movements. They all perform at the same time but each dancer starts at a different point of the sequence -

Movements		Dancers' Numbers	
1	-	4	(e.g. Number 4 dancer starts on Number 1 movement and works through the sequence from 1 to 6)
2	-	3	
3	-	6	
4	-	2	(Number 2 dancer starts performing Number 4 movement and works through the sequence from 4 to 3)
5	-	1	
6	-	5	

6. Three Group Canon (see Figures 13 and 14). The As start to move, the Bs start their movement 1 when the As reach movement 4, then the As and Bs all join in with the Cs and perform in unison. This happens when the As reach movement 6 and the Bs reach movement 2. In other words, at this point As and Bs revert to movement 1 and perform the whole six movements together.

Figure 13

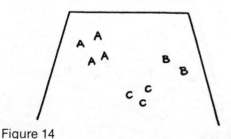

Figure 14

7. Canoned Crossing (see Figure 15). The front line starts. When they have crossed the line behind, this motivates the second line to join in. When the second line crosses the third line, the third line joins in and so on.

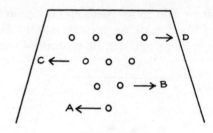

Figure 15

When choosing the most appropriate way of canoning, as with any choice of temporal or spatial structuring, bear in mind the following polarities:

monotony	——	confusion
decoration	——	affectation
simplicity	——	chaos.

Experimental Task Using Canon and Unison Movement Within a Particular Design

This exercise is an improvisation task for early stages of choreography to experiment with ways of canoning the chosen movement vocabulary. It is an excellent way of helping the choreographer to find which movements are most suited to canon and which to unison work.

Exercise: Teach the dancers the movements of the dance. Then ask them to stand in a circle one behind the other. Number them round from 1 to 6. (Each member must take note of the person who is directly in front of him because this is the person to copy.) Then arrange the dancers into some sort of group design facing various directions. It is more interesting if group members do not stand directly next to the person whom they will copy. They must, however, be able to see that person. Number 1 starts to move, using the previously taught movements as the basis for his dance. Number 2 begins to move one beat behind Number 1 copying Number 1's movements exactly, then Number 3, one beat behind

2, and so on. When Number 1, the leader, shouts 'unison' all members shift their focus to the leader and start to move at exactly the same time as him/her with the same movement. The leader can also shout 'close' during travelling motifs, and the group members must then move in closer towards each other. Watch this improvising process, and then select the particular designs and ways of canon and unison which have 'worked'. Then use this to assemble a finished choreography. An additional instruction of '3 canon movements followed by 3 unison movements and then repeat' can provide further structure in the experimental and choreographic stages.

Note: It is vital that the leader includes pauses in this exercise so that members can 'catch up'. Be firm. If the progression is going wrong in the experimental stage (i.e. if the dancers are watching the leader when they are meant to be watching their preceding number), stop the group, correct the fault at its source, and ask the leader to start again.

10. The Role of Properties, The Set and Costume in Choreography

Properties

Props can add to the design or the expression of a movement. Props can be used literally as the objects they are or they can be used in a more abstract fashion as extensions to the body, creating additional body lines to add clarity or decoration to a movement. Or props can be used like tap shoes to heighten the accenting in a phrase. Many cane dances for example use the cane to make a sound to highlight the syncopated phrase. If props are to be used as an integral part of a dance, it is vital that they are used in the very first rehearsal, otherwise some of the choreography may well have to be redone. It is impossible to visualise all the potential possibilities and problems of dancing with a prop.

Straight Line Props

There are various props which can add a clear straight line to a movement, or can emphasise the angularity of a position, for example canes, umbrellas, walking sticks, feather dusters (see Figures 1, 2, 3 and 4). The use of a straight line prop is often an excellent way of tidying up body design in a group of dancers who have little dance training or weak technique and therefore whose body lines tend to be spatially inexact.

Figure 2

The identity of the prop can change during the dance. Movements where it is used in an abstract manner can follow movements where it is used literally. Indeed there can be a succession of different representations. The spectator can easily adapt to such changing identities. The cane in a number like 'Putting on the Ritz' (*Top Hat*), for example, can be used as a walking stick then played as if it was

Figure 1

Figure 3

Figure 4

Figure 6

a guitar, then used as an umbrella, then as an additional line to complement that of the thigh, then as a sword with a fencing movement, ending up as a naughty dog on a leash. Using

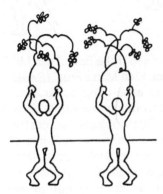

Figure 5a

two props, one in each hand, can be very effective. They can be crossed or remain apart from each other (see Figure 5a and b). If there is only one prop, the spare hand can be used on occasions as added decoration. An example of this is shown in Figure 6.

Figure 5b

Some straight line props can be used effectively by a large group. A ladder, for example, can highlight the design of the line of dancers. They can step into it, carry it by their sides or put their heads through it. Or a group may form a cross or star with sticks or canes in the air or make one long 'cane' by standing side by side and holding their props at the same height.

Figure 7

Cloth and Clothes

Cloth has flowing qualities and a sense of movement unlike straight line props. Towels, shawls, scarves, can all decorate a design. In Figure 7 for example, dancers have their backs to the audience and rub their backs with bath towels using a syncopated rhythm. Remember that the flow of the cloth should not be used as substitute for the clear structuring of movement temporally and structurally. There are so many poor dances which use bits of floating chiffon together with similarly undisciplined arm wafting! It is a mistake to assume that the flowing qualities of some materials are so pleasing just as they are that they do not need careful choreographic structuring.

Putting on Clothes

The dancer can mime putting on clothes or can put them on in actuality using exaggerated rhythmic movements. In Figure 8, for example, dancers are all putting a shirt on in unison. Syncopated gesture to show the tidying of clothing in a group, for example, straightening hats or collars, polishing shoes, is effective. It is pleasing for two groups to co-exist, both performing different activities with clothes. One group for example may be swinging beads whilst another puts on and takes off their headgear as could be used in a number like 'Aquarius' from the musical *Hair*.

Figure 8

Hats

Putting on hats and taking them off as part of the movement is demonstrated in Figure 9. A dancer can hold a hat in front of him with both arms bringing it away or towards the body. He may balance the hat on a cane. A group may use their hats to form a wall for them to hide behind. Canoning with hats; for example, a line of people taking off their hats in ripple canon often presents a delightful picture.

Figure 9

Other Objects

Smaller objects which cannot strongly affect the lines of a body design due to their size, can however be used to add an element of decoration to an otherwise plain movement. They may be used to exaggerate mannerisms. For example a cigarette holder can be held in an affected way and the smoking can become a whole body movement, as would be effective

Figure 10

in a number like 'Take Back Your Mink' (*Guys and Dolls*) or 'Rich Man's Frug' (*Sweet Charity*). Similarly the wine glass or tankard can add delightful decoration to a whole body drinking movement. Such objects can create interesting air patterns. As shown in Figure 10, waiters in a song such as 'Hello Dolly' (*Hello Dolly*) can use trays of glasses (glued to the tray of course) to produce beautiful swooping, curving, spiralling air patterns. If any carried object is big enough, it is delightful to hide the entire body behind it and travel across the stage totally masked, perhaps following an unmasked dancer in this way.

Below is a list of objects and suggestions of how they could be incorporated into a choreography:

Hat Boxes	- Stand on them, stack them
Umbrellas	- Put it up, walk round it, kick it, catch it, open and close it (see Figure 11)
Balls	- Throw them, juggle with them
Mirror	- Polish it, look into it
Flags	- Waved, use as sail for ship (see Figure 12)
Rubber Rings	- Throw them, stack them

Figure 11

Telephones	– Dial, pick up the receiver (with the whole body), get tangled in the wires
Balloons	– Bounce, rotate, wriggle, pass under the legs
Books	– Bury the head in one, wear one on the head
Camera	– Held in front of the face or between the legs (the eccentric tourist)
Fans	– Hide behind them, open and close them
Dustbins	– Carry them, use the lids as steering wheels
Linen Baskets, etc.	– Wheels, ship's wheel, get inside them, roll in them, use them as a vehicle e.g. a punt with a broom.

chairs put together can become a vehicle, a bus or train. Three people can sit on each other's laps on the same chair to make a human tower. Or chairs can simply be used to add lines to the body (Figure 13). A group

Figure 13

may sit down on chairs in ripple canon. In Figure 14 the chairs are a delightful addition to the set. The seated group are very close and as contrast the individuals on the high scaffolding are spread out and standing up. Sitting

Figure 12

Furniture

1. The Chair. The performer can move around, over, under, above or through a chair. Chairs can be carried, sat on, stood on, laid across, balanced on, tipped up, turned over, used for acrobatic purposes. One performer can drag another off stage sitting on a chair. Several

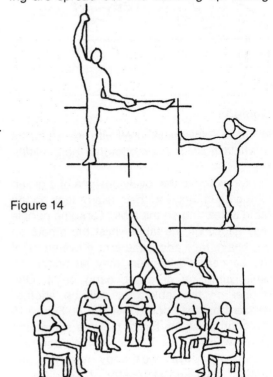

Figure 14

down routines such as 'Sit Down You're Rocking The Boat' (*Guys and Dolls*), 'The Triplet's Number' (*Bandwagon*) and 'The Bingo Song' (*Beowulf*), offer much potential for hand, head, torso and feet isolations, for example, crossing and uncrossing the legs, flexing the feet, crossing and uncrossing the arms.

2. The Bench. This item of furniture has the added value of being able to easily accommodate more than one person. Again, three people crossing and uncrossing legs on a bench is delightful, or use the built in levels of a bench by three people sitting on the back of the bench, three on the actual seat, and maybe three on the floor in front of the bench. Alternatively one dancer could lie full length on the bench whilst the others lean over the top. Settees have an added bonus of being softer! Dancers can sit on a settee, topple it backwards whilst still sitting on it and then maybe perform a backwards somersault off it (with a cushioned landing) to complete the effect.

Figure 15

3. Tables. Tables when used with chairs present a whole host of choreographic possibilities's.

Try for example the lovely designs of a group sitting on chairs with their fists or legs on the table or leaning on the table. Or some people may dance on the table whilst the others on the chairs may adopt the arm movements of the dancers. Or dancers may sit under the table, jump on or off it, hang on it. One dancer on the table may pull up another dancer from the floor to join him. In Figure 15 the chorus use the bar or table as something to sprawl over. This provides a lovely contrast, the flopping asymetrical body designs to the straight lines and symmetry of the piece of furniture.

4. Beds. Use beds as trampolines, swimming pools, vehicles, a desert island and a space ship.

5. Hat Stands. Carry people on them. Use them for a human sacrifice (see Figure 16).

Figure 16

6. Clothes Rails. If these have wheels, ride on them, crash them, hang on them, vault over them.

Always refer closely to both lyrics and dialogue to think of any other possible transformations of furniture into other things.

Using Intergral Parts of the Set

1. Steps. Steps have the attraction of built-in levels. The neatness of the stacking can be emphasised by a neat body design. For example, people simply sitting on the different steps singing with their feet and hands together can be highly effective in songs such as 'Safety

Figure 17

in Numbers' (*The Boyfriend*), 'Happy Endings' (*New York, New York*), and 'I'll Build a Stairway to Paradise' (*An American in Paris*). When using steps in a dance, the choreographer can exploit the exhilaration of height, the danger of falling, or the dancers can perform careful balancing acts. A group may walk in unison up and down the steps with their backs to the audience, then suddenly turn. They may travel in a pattern such as two steps up, one down, three up, four down, one up and one to the side. In Figure 17 the couple walk up and down the steps, crossing over constantly in the process.

Figure 17

2. Step Ladders. These provide different levels. Two people on either side on a ladder can produce a symmetrical or asymmetrical design, depending on which step they choose. They may walk up and down together or at different times and onto different steps to produce a constant shift of level (Figure 18).

Figure 18

3. Arches. Dancers may move in and out of arches like weathermen. They invite the interest of alternation that is an A B A B A B situation (Figure 19)

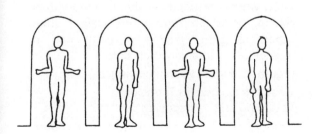

Figure 19

4. Poles, Pillars and Lamp Posts. Dancers can slide down these, wrap their legs around them, lean on them, or jump onto them (see Figure 20). Unison work, one dancer per pole, is often delightful.

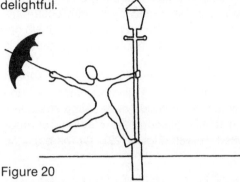

Figure 20

5. Bannisters. Again dancers can slide down them, lean on them, poke their heads or limbs through the holes (e.g. 'Do a Deer' (*The Sound of Music*); 'Big Spender' (*Sweet Charity*)).

6. Walls, Hedges etc. Dancers can jump onto them or hide behind them whilst sporadically arms or legs reappear (e.g. 'Make 'Em Laugh' (*Singing in the Rain*).

7. Curtains. These provide opportunities for disguise and hiding places (see Figure 21). Lumps in the curtain, particularly moving lumps, always provide amusement.

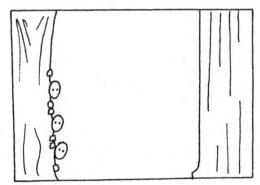

Figure 21

8. Ramps. These can achieve exciting effects if used to run up or down. Do not, however, choreograph turns on ramps unless the gradient is very slight, otherwise dancers will lose their sense of balance.

Costume

Study the script carefully to establish what the dancers will need in terms of costume for each dance number. Stunning choreographic designs can be ruined by certain costumes. For example, the choreographer may have designed a split leap only to find the dancer is supposed to be wearing a tight skirt. Or he may have spent hours perfecting a superb arm design only to discover later that the costume is a multitude of dangling streamers which totally obscure the carefully choreographed curve! (Figure 22). Or perhaps he

Figure 22

wanted to create a unified group with identical positions, an effect which would be quickly destroyed if all the dancers were to wear different costumes, some with thick sleeves,

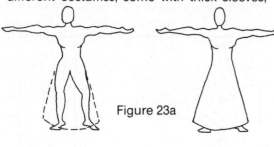

Figure 23a

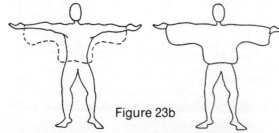

Figure 23b

some with no sleeves, some with shirts and trousers. Figures 23 a & b illustrate how in circumstances such as these, group members

would no longer appear to be all standing in the same position.

If a choreographer has prior knowledge of exactly what a costume will be like, he can actually choreograph it in to the design of a movment. For example the lines of the cloak drawn in Figure 24 can add an element of decoration to a plain movement. A full skirt can

Figure 24

become part of a movement. It can be moved in a figure of eight or up and down to reveal layers of petticoats. If costumes are to become integral to the movement design, ensure that they are practised with and well in advance.

Costume Colours

Colours have many emotional associations. Red is a warm colour and can be used to symbolise ideas such as blood, fire, the spoils of war, vulgarity. Red, yellow and orange can excite and give off energy. These colours have short wave lengths, thus can be quickly registered by the spectator. In contrast blue and green are colder, less intense colours and often tend to recede. Blue is associated with calm moods, water, sky, nature. White is appropriate to emphasise purity, innocence, the spiritual or ethereal.

It is important for the choreographer to know which colours draw attention more than others, or which have more 'weight' than others. A group may be strengthened in impact by the intensity of its colour.

Figure 25, Figure 26 in following section

Costume Colours in Terms of Grouping and Juxtaposing

Colour can be used to distinguish one group from another, or one individual from another. Man tends to refer to colour quickly in an identifying or categorising process. In a situation like that outlined in Figure 25, it is likely that the spectator will register that all the 'greens' are performing the same movement, despite the fact that they are not standing together. If two different colours are juxtaposed, as for example in the splitting of greens and blues in Figure 25, the result is likely to be pleasing. If, however, three or more colours

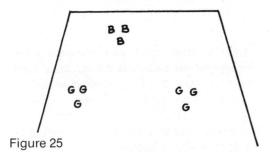

Figure 25

are juxtaposed as shown in Figure 26, the effect will tend to be visually disruptive in terms of order and grouping. Here the balance and symmetry have been thrown into disarray and the colour variation is too diverse to be taken in comfortably. If, however, a choreographer wishes there to be colour interaction and merger between groups, then everyone wearing a different colour can produce a wash of colour on stage. Tie-dying costumes, or everyone wearing a slightly different shade of the same basic costume will create an even softer merger. There is a general rule to have only two major colours on stage or to have

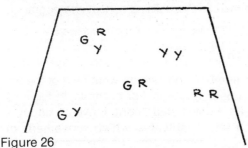

Figure 26

everyone in a different colour. Any in-between stages, for example three colours, or four, or five, begin to look messy and garish in a large group, regardless of the compactness of grouping and clarity of body design. Think of your everyday clothes sense to validate this. Wearing two colours, for example, a brown

skirt and blue blouse, will usually appear suitably complementary, but more than two, for example, yellow socks with a brown skirt, blue blouse, will often seem too much. Extremes, however, such as rainbow patterns in jumpers or skirts are often attractive. Effective two colour combinations on stage are:

Red and Blue
Red and Purple
Blue and Green
Light Pink and Light Blue
Yellow and Blue.

Be aware that juxtaposing colours of different intensities, hues or tones, choosing for example to use a light pastel blue for one group juxtaposed with a group wearing dark shiny red, will produce a state of asymmetry.

A whole stage of people wearing the same colour of costume can have great impact due again to the fascination of duplication. Slightly different shades of the same colour can have a similar effect. Consider using ultraviolet lighting with some costumes. Lighting white gloves, white ties and white socks is often very effective.

Coloured Costumes and Coloured Set

Be aware of the colours in the back drop or set. Sometimes it is both pleasing and appropriate to include in the costumes some of the colours or textures of the material used in the set. In a 'space' environment like the one in the musical *Dazzle* for example, tinfoil on the back cloth can be echoed in the hats of the spacemen. Too much imitation of exact material, pattern and colour used in the set can act as camouflage, the figures merging into the background. On some occasions the matching of set to costumes will seem too pretty and resemble Sanderson's bedroom matching curtain and duvet sets. It is, however, always important to consider the effect of the set on the costume. For example:

1. Some light costumes may suddenly look very dark against certain sets, that is any colour will look darker if set against a white set or back cloth.
2. Light colours seem more intense and are given clearer outlines if placed against a black background.

11. Pre-Planning and Rehearsing Choreography

Pre-Planning on Paper

Much useful prelimenary work can be done before meeting the dancers. Neglecting to pre-plan for choreography would be rather like thinking up the lyrics of the songs when meeting the singers. There are many ways of pre-visualising choreographic effects, by working things out on paper. Patterns which are visually pleasing on paper are likely to be pleasing visually when translated into group-ings of dancers on stage, whereas boring or

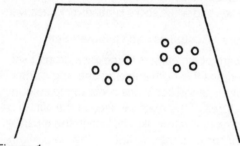

Figure 1

messy patterns on paper are often doomed to failure when transferred to the stage. In Figure 1 for example this design on paper is likely to produce blocking problems and to be boring due to the lack of depth. Therefore preliminary paper work can help to ensure that potential problems are foreseen and avoided. Paper work can guarantee that in the choreography there is:

1. use of sufficient depth in terms of groupings
2. an avoidance of masking
3. interesting design of grouping
4. no visual bombardment or multifocal prob-lems, when many different groups share the stage.

(This latter point can sometimes be deceptive on paper. A design may look tidy on paper but too cluttered when put into effect on stage. In plotting the dance with the dancers, if the design is too cluttered, merely subtract a few people or groups from the design).

5. an ease of transitions of groups. We suggest using buttons as opposed to drawings for this, moving them around to try out the effect of a certain transition. Coloured buttons are particularly useful if the choreo-grapher is grouping by colours and wishes to see the colour effects of an interchange of members from one group to another.

If there is a preference to use accepted notation techniques, it is possible to quickly learn a few basic Labanotation movements (see *Labanotation* by Ann Hutchinson), other-wise personal hieroglyphics are very adequate. Below are listed suggested ways of notating and therefore visualising certain choreographic patterns:

Canon

The numbers indicate on what beat of the bar each person moves. For example, in Figure 2 the As, futhest stage right, move on count 3. Each letter indicates which movement or

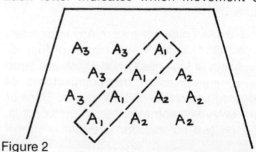

Figure 2

movement sequence the dancer is performing. For example, all those indicated with a letter A dance sequence A. In Figure 3:

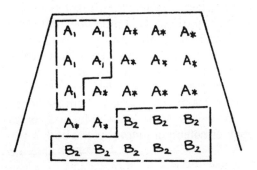

Figure 3

As start on count 1 with sequence A

Bs start on count 2 with sequence B

A* hold the first position throughout.

Syncopated Stepping Patterns

It is possible to compose syncopated phrases, simply by jotting down numbers, dashes and the word or symbol 'and' - for example:

1 & 2 & 3 4 & 5 - 6 & 7 - 8 - etc.

It may have taken much longer to think up this by standing around in front of the mirror, moving the feet around. The phrase can be given more details by more notated signs, for example:

$T^1/_4 = ^1/_4$ turn

$T^1/_2 = ^1/_2$ turn

l = left foot

r = right foot

4/4	$T^1/_4$		$T^1/_2$		$T^1/_4$		$T^1/_2$	
	1	& 2	& 3	4	& 5	- 6	& 7	- 8
	l	r l	r	l r	l r	l	r l	r

The 'Chinese Take-away' Method of Building Up an Order of Movements For a Dance

One way of structuring a dance and positioning movements chosen is to number each movement. There may for example be 16 movements (possibly all variations on the same theme to be performed by a group of five dancers). A way of ensuring an interesting juxtaposition of such groups of this number and of the different movements, to include repetition and development of the material is to notate as follows:

2 × No 16 & 3 × No 8

(2 dancers perform number 16 movement, and 3 dancers perform number 8)

5 × No 8

(All 5 dancers perform number 8 movement)

1 × No 3 & 4 × No 7

(1 dancer performs movement number 3 whilst 4 perform number 7 movement)

5 × No 16

(All dancers perform number 16 movement)

1 × No 11 & 2 × No 14 & 2 × No 13

(1 dancer performs number 11 movement, whilst 2 perform number 14 and 2 perform number 13)

In the initial stages this notation does not need to be given much thought. Numbers can be jotted down quickly and arbitrarily then tried out as an experimental stage of choreography. Those movements that work can then be preserved and incorporated in the choreography whilst the weaker movements can be discarded.

Rehearsing the Dancers

Warn the dancers of the necessity of experimentation in the initial rehearsal sessions. In other words that there may well be a need to change steps and positions the dancers have already learnt. No choreographer should be expected to set his work in the first rehearsal and then not to change it. Firstly this would rule out the choreographer using inspirational ideas for movements and ideas that may occur to him during the rehearsal. Secondly, even extensive and thorough pre-planning cannot hope to forsee all problems, which the early rehearsal and plotting stages will throw up. Try, however, to give the dancers a clear estimate on which session there will be no more changes made, so that they do not feel exploited or generally messed about.

Design and Spacing Precision

Help the dancers to take responsibility for making the necessary adjustments and corrections to spacing inaccuracies. Stop the music when spatial positioning is poor in terms of the original instructions given to the dancers. Do not tell the dancers how to correct it, but ask them to work out for themselves what is wrong and who should move towards or away from whom. Only intervene if their corrections are wrong.

It may be necessary sometimes to place markers on the stage floor (little pieces of tape) to mark where a dancer in a key position in a group formation is to stand. All the other dancers can orient themselves from this central person. The use of markers can prevent problems particularly common to the large group design where, for example, the curtain rises only to reveal a group intended to be placed centre stage, slightly over to one side.

The Art of Polishing Unison Work

Be prepared to take hours over this. The spectator quickly registers unison work which is not together, and sees it as untidy and, therefore, unsatisfying. However small deviations may seem, one head slightly turned in the wrong direction, one hand with fingers apart where all other dancers have their fingers together, they are noticed even by the untrained eye, as is the one singer singing a flat note in a choir of people with perfect pitch. The 'almost symmetrical' or the 'slightly imperfect right angle' simply will not do. Little imperfections in unison work often mark the difference between amateur and professional shows.

Extremeties

By looking closely at the feet and hands of a group who are supposed to be dancing in unison, it is often possible to see a vast array of different positions. Choreographers seem either to forget these body parts or to regard them as unnecessary detail. It is important to decide upon the exact distance between one foot and the other and to provide the dancers with a clear visual estimate. For example, feet in position 'X' should be placed one and a half foot lengths apart, or hands in position 'Y' where the arms are above the head, should be placed the width of a head apart. With feet, decide upon the exact angle of each foot in each position, selecting from a range of parallel to a 180° turn out. Common questions to ask with hands positions are as follows: Are the palms supposed to be turned towards the ceiling or towards the audience or down towards the floor? Are fingers together or apart? Is the thumb held apart from the fingers? Are the hands by the sides of the body or held together behind or in front of the body?

Activities

In rehearsing such activities as jumps, turns, falls, etc., think in terms of size, speed, preparation and finish, and use of individual body parts. With a jump, for example, how high is the jump to be? How low is the preliminary bend? How far are the legs apart? Or with a sway, is the movement initiated in the ribs or hips? Is it to be a successive swaying, one part of the body moving after another, or are all the body parts to move simultaneously?

Polishing Work with Props

If a unison group is using props provide exact instructions as to how they should be held. Consider such things as how far is the object from the body? Are the arms outstretched or bent? Is the object opposite the face or chest or hips? Are the fingers apart when holding the object or together? Are the hands held around the top of the object or around the sides? Is one hand at the top and the other one at the bottom (see Figure 4). If a prop is changed from one hand to another, how is this done? If a prop is rotated, a cane for example, is the circular motion ⟲ or ⟳ ?

Figure 4

Focusing and Projection

To ensure that performers project whilst dancing, ask them to THINK BIG AND HIGH. Heads and eyes need to be held higher than normal to give a sense of uplift and confidence. Just as everything on stage needs to be big and bold, props and scenery designs for example, so each movement needs to be exaggerated and fully extended. See that there is no unofficial eye contact between performers. This can cause distracting visual lines for the spectator. Clarify the eye focus of every single movement in the final stages of rehearsal. Decide whether each dancer should be looking forward or to the side or to a certain diagonal and for how long. Use objects on the back auditorium wall - exit signs, a clock, for common focal points. However polished the movement is itself, if all the eyes in a unison group are focusing in different directions, there will be an untidy feel to the group. Draw attention to fidgeting early on. Performers are often not aware that they have a 'pulling-down-leotard' habit.

Preparation for Handling the Mishap

Before the performance, talk to the dancers about ways of coping with possible mishaps, for example, someone's skirt falling off; one dancer bumping into another; someone falling over; one dancer speeding up the tempo or forgetting a movement phrase in unison work.

Rehearsing with Music

Find the pulse of the music. Do not try counting complex metric changes in a piece of music that changes from 3/4 to 6/8 to 9/12 every few bars for example. Attempting to familiarise the dancer with these time signatures would only make unnecessary demands on her movement memory. If the music is nonmetric but the dance is intended to be metrically phrased, use a metronome in the early rehearsal stages. It is surprising how soon the metre and tempo can be internalised by the dancers. As a safety device use a competent dancer as a steadier. Other dancers should refer to her if they worry that they are losing their rhythm or slowing down or speeding up. However if she goes wrong, impress on the whole group that they will have to go along with her.

Do one rehearsal which consists solely of learning musical cues, and practising coming in with the music at the right time. Dancers should be in no doubt with each different musical number, as to whether they start to dance before the music or during it. If the latter is the case, they should be sure how many beats of musical introduction there are before their first movement in each danced number. Sometimes they will need to be aware of word cues as opposed to or as well as musical cues.

Appendix I

About Appendix I

The appendix consists of examples of the pre-planning stages for five dance numbers: it exemplifies notes a choreographer may have made about a 'number' before meeting the dancers and which he is likely to take with him to his first rehearsal. Each example presupposes that the 'fictitious' choreographer will have (a) familiarised himself with the musical; (b) read both the score and the text; (c) listened to a recording of the music for the number many times; (d) taped the track; (e) worked out the number of beats available for each line or section (using the pause button on the recorder); and (f) read the lyrics through many times - all before sitting down with pen and paper. Also each example presupposes that during his writing of notes the choreographer has had the score, libretto, tape of the music, set design and costume designs at hand.

The five numbers have been chosen to illustrate different choreographic problems:

1. *'Come One' from Act I* Beowulf *by Ken Pickering & Keith Cole*

This number must incorporate a chase between two people. There are various instructions written into the lyrics. There is a sung dialogue between a soloist and chorus group. Illustrative gesture is clearly appropriate. There are two choruses which have a very different tempo and rhythm from the verses.

2. *'Potiphar' from Act I* Joseph and the Amazing Technicolor Dreamcoat *by Tim Rice & Andrew Lloyd Webber*

This number includes a major development of the plot. This development can be dealt with effectively through both dance and mime. Clear instructions as to the various 'dance events' are written in the lyrcs. There are six members of the male chorus, two chorus women, Mrs. Potiphar, Joseph and Potiphar himself. The choreographic relationship between the main characters and the chorus members needs to be handled carefully. There are distinct tempo and rhythm changes between the verses and the choruses.

3. *'Bingo Song' from Act II* Beowulf *by Ken Pickering & Keith Cole*

This number must revolve around a game of Bingo. It should also contain visual humour. There are two groups, one of old ladies and one of hostesses and one soloist, 'mother'. These parties stay on stage throughout the number and must remain fairly separate. Thus the choreographer must devise ways of avoiding visual competition between them.

4. *'Olklahoma!' Finale number from* Olklahoma *by Richard Rodgers & Oscar Hammerstein*

A production number, the choreography of which must generate energy and warm communication with the audience as the Finale. It must include spectacle and an air of celebration. The relationship between the main couple (the man is the main solo singer) and the chorus needs devising.

5. *'Light of the World' and preceding dialogue - end number in Act I of* Godspell *by Stephen Schwartz*

This number has a small cast of ten with several solo singers. The choreography must show the togetherness of the group. There is not much space as the set limits the dancing area. The music includes various instrumental breaks and changes in tempi.

The numbers also illustrate different methods of pre-planning:

1. 'Come One'   - Design/Vocabulary Division
2. 'Potiphar'   - Design/Vocabulary Division
3. 'Bingo Song'   - The Table
4. 'Olklaholma!'   - Sectioning of Events
5. 'Light of the World' - Line by line planning with floor patterns

(We hope that when you choreograph you try out some or all of these different methods of pre-planning to find the one most suited to your way of working.)

How to use the Appendix

The appendix is designed to demonstrate how the book can be used practically and, if you wish, rather like an 'à la carte' menu from which to select and adapt ideas. The numbers we have chosen to choreograph, therefore, often refer to illustrations from the text. If, for example, 'C8, 15' is notated, this indicates that the idea demonstrated in Chapter 8, Figure 15 has been incorporated in the dance number. In order to use the appendix effectively therefore, we advise the reader to turn back to the appropriate part of the text when illustrations are referred to. We have deliberately not incorporated new illustrations at this stage (apart from floor plans for the *Godspell* number which are necessary to demonstrate a specific choreographic method) since we consider the main body of the book to be a comprehensive guide to choreography.

Other uses of shorthand are outlined below:

    l   - left
    r   - right
    DSL   - down stage left
    USR   - up stage right
    CS   - centre stage

All lyrics are in square brackets - [Take her on your knee]

Note: It is assumed that the stage is 20 feet by 20 feet (6 metres by 6 metres) for each example.

'Come One' (Music 20) Act I Beowulf by Ken Pickering & Keith Cole

Choreographic Method I - Design/Vocabulary Division

The design and use of space for each verse is plannned *before* the vocabulary rather like painting a picture and colouring it in afterwards. With this method the design may need to be adapted or changed when the movements and steps are chosen as indeed vocabulary should in no way be subservient to design. The choeographer here has by and large outlined various alternatives for each section. Each of these will be tried out in rehearsal to decide which is the most effective.

Comments about this method. Some people find the design/vocabulary division unhelpful and prefer instead to plan the two simultaneously. Laying out possible alternatives in pre-planning notes is particularly useful for a choreographer who tends not to see new possibilities or adaptations of what he has set, when he is actually in the rehearsal room.

The Choreography Plan

Initial Reactions and Thoughts about Choreographic Needs

1. People are rowdy and drunk - need energetic movement, a lot of space, travelling,

2. There is a table on stage, otherwise a lot of open space available. Table can be moved - maybe use it for 'level' variation?

3. From the designs, costumes do not seem in any way restrictive in terms of body line and movement activity - tight fitting and stretch fabric.

4. Lyrics - great possibilities for extensive use of illustrative gesture.

5. There are various inherent choreographic instructions in the song (e.g. [Join the ring], [Take her on your knee]).

6. Chorus is repeated once

7. Decide what sort of chase it is to be before planning use of space, floor patterns. Who is chasing whom? How many people are involved? Blindfolds? Children's game?

8. High spots - are [Got You] and [Hey Hey

Hey Hey] - (happens twice each chorus)?

9. Obe, chorus, and chasing couple - therefore in effect three co-existing parties to choreograph at times. Problems with visual competition.

10. Activity number, chorus involved in the events on stage, therefore front on movement not appropriate (side and diagonal facings better).

Come One

A. General Sequence of Events
B. Design and Use of Space
    a) Verse I
    b) Chorus I
    c) Verse II
    d) Verse III
    e) Chorus II
C. Possible Spatial Transitions
D. Vocabulary
    a) Illustrative gesture throughout
    b) Possible movements for each section

A. General Sequence of Events

Verse I   - illustrative gesture section, little travelling, unison group and soloist (Obe - jester)

Chorus I - circle dance and chase, travelling

d) Obe at the end of a line of revellers
e) Obe conversing with different clumps of revellers.

Design for First Chorus - The Chase
(Lyrics [And the she-wolf . . . — Now.])

Possible Options:

a) Chase (involving a number of people) going on around a strong diagonal line of static revellers who simply perform hand gestures (this allows for the chase to comprise wild and energetic movements, as the singing can be left to those on the diagonal line) (C6, 1).

b) Chase happens around a wedge formation of static revellers (C5, 12).

c) Chase centre stage whilst static revellers are around the outside of it in a semi-circle, therefore having a framing effect (C6, 21) or in various clumps (C2, 12).

d) [Join the ring, join the ring] - 'woman tries to reach the centre of a circle' - (stage direction) to catch her mate who is hiding there.

There may be two circles of revellers, one small, one large, travelling in opposite directions, or three circles (C6, 19; C6, 20) the couple running in and out, around and through these.

e) Chase could adopt the formation and travelling patterns of a children's game like 'cat and mouse' or 'fox and geese'.

f) Circles could develop out of a male/female ensemble (C5, 35b).

Try all these separately and in combination in first rehearsal.

Design for Verse II (Lyrics [One, two, three . . . — Got You]
Remember this ends in a high point - 'Got You'.

Possible options:

a) Only the main couple continue the chase - no revellers joining it. Woman chasing man through static 'distant' group. Going in and out, they occasionally touch the stationary singers, hide behind them, jump over them, spin them around (C2, 14).

b) Formal, close group (static) sing and perform illustrative gesture USL (on table or rostra). Chase continues in front of singers with only a small group (e.g. four dancers and the couple) - DSR They are a 'distant' group (C5, 16).

c) Got You! - the woman should catch the man - in an easily seen position - higher level from other revellers if possible (e.g. on table).

Design for Verse III (Lyrics [Come now fill your . . . — prey]
End of chase. Need a contrast here, a rest from hectic travelling.

Static group all in unison. Obe joins in.

Possible options:

a) Levelled clump - hand on shoulders - moving bodies forward/back and side to side (C3, 22 - one group not two as in this diagram).

b) More than one group - identical movements but each group having a variation in level, direction, number in group etc. (C7, 18, 19, 20, 21, 22).

Verse II - illustrative gesture group with the chase continuing between a couple, completion of the chase.

Verse III - a close group - unison movement - Obe part of this (illustrative gesture).

Chorus II - repeat of circle dance and chase.

(The sections parallel the change of tempo in the music - the faster chorus sections have more travelling, the slower verse sections are more static.)

B. Design and use of Space

Verse I

1. Start USR - (possible on and around table which could be pushed there during previous section) - close clump with variation in body levels moving and spreading out DSC after a time (C5, 11).

2. The spreading out should avoid straight line floor patterns so use curves or diagonal lines in this part. Eye focus should be on each other, not out front to the audience.

3. Interaction between soloist (Jester Obe) and revellers group. It is probably best to keep Obe and chorus group close together - remember stage direction in text: 'Obe stirs them to greater exuberance all the while' therefore Obe probably needs to move among revellers some of the time.

Possible options
Try all these separately and in combination in first rehearsal

a) Revellers following Obe around (C2, 1(b))

b) Obe DSL of the revellers group whilst all dance on the spot (C2, 7)

c) Obe in the middle of a line of revellers, as the odd one out - different movement. His costume will also make him stand out (C2, 9)

Design for Chorus II
Possible options:

a) Effective to use the repeat in the lyrics and music therefore chorus II could be the same as chorus I.

b) Same as chorus I with slight variation, for example different movement activity on the four 'Heys' or different circle formations.

C. Possible Spatial Transitions

a) If verse one finishes in two groups - move into circles via a crossing curve (C8, 3).

b) At end of first chase 'concertina' into a group for verse II (C8, 5).

c) Possible transition for end of chorus I to start verse II would be to move out of a circle into a semicircle (C8, 8) or from a circle into line (C8, 20).

d) If a static group in chorus I is used the chase can run through it to form one group for verse III (C9, 4).

e) To break up 'levelled clump' in verse III so as to form in chorus II use two arc lines crossing (C8, 24b).

f) Transition to dialogue at the end of dance photo finish - allow for applause, then each dancer talks to person next to them and picks up glass to resume drinking during Hrothgar's [Now we have feasted well] etc.

D. Vocabulary
(Teach steps before formation positions at rehearsals)

Words appropriate to be used for illustrative gesture:

Obe	Come one, come all
Chorus	Join the rev'llers in this hall
Obe	Eat, drink, dance, sing*
Chorus	Now's the time to have a *fling*
Obe	All your cares are gone
Chorus	As the dance goes on and on
Obe	Let the *music play**
Chorus	And the she-wolf find her prey - hey, hey, hey, hey. Let us sing, let us sing - hey, hey, hey, hey Join the ring, join the ring now
Obe	One two three four

Chorus	Do not *open every door*
Obe	Five six seven eight
Chorus	Why's your *lover always late?*
Both	Can she *sew* and cook
Chorus	*Wash* a jerkin in the brook
Both	Hey, hey, hey got you!

This song continues antiphonally

Obe	Come now *fill your glass*
Chorus	Find yourself a comely lass
	Take her on your knee
	With your *purse** she will be free.
	Life's a passing game
	Join the ring and say your name
	Let the she-wolf find her prey - hey,
	hey . . .

Italicised words all lend themselves to illustrative gesture. Due to the fast tempo of the music, however, the dance would probably appear too static and lose some of its flow if there was a great deal of illustrative gesture. Therefore it is probably wise not to use words marked with an asterisk to cut down illustrative gesture to a bare minimum.

Ideas for Illustrative Gesture
Verse I

If 'clumps' design used, each clump could perform an illustrative gesture for one of the following words (equivalent to C1, 2):

Group A -	*'Eat'*	canoned gestures -
Group B -	*'Drink'*	in position on
Group C -	*'Dance'*	completion of each
Group D -	*'Sing'*	action

[Now's the time to have a fling] - wild jumps in unison - or if in groups - each group performs a different jump (try all the jumps in C3, 57 to see which seem most pleasing in unison).

Verse II
(Appropriate if design idea adopted of static group performing illustrative gesture in unison in the middle of, or surrounding, the chase)

[Do not open every door]
Syncopated 'unlocking door, turning door knob, pushing door open' sequence - using whole body.

[Why's your lover always late?]
Synchronised head shaking and finger shaking movement whilst bobbing up and down and scowling.

[Can she sew and cook]
Sewing mime - syncopation as the cotton gets stuck - torso involved in a side to side sway.

[Wash a jerkin in the brook]
Washing and wringing action - symmetrical arms - knee bend.

Verse III
[Come now fill your glass]

$$(\&1)$$
Syncopated gesture phrase, e.g. of filling glass,
$$(2) \qquad\qquad (\&4)$$
knocking glasses together and drinking (partner work)
† four beats (&1 - 2 - &4) freezing on the '-' dashes.

[Take her on your knee]
Man spins lady towards him to sit on his knee. (All these ideas are designed for unison work).

Possible Movements for Each Section
Verse I

1) Starting position - drunk over the table (C10, 15).

2) Jester energetically jumps on table during first line, causing others to fall on the floor and wake up (or generally scatter with his jump - clearly motivated movement plus reaction).

3) On [Join the revellers in the hall]
       A   B   C   D   E   F   G
canon standing up raising imaginary glasses (levelled clusters of revellers A — G)

4) Jester *Obe* - fast movement 'Puck like jumps' (try out jumps C3, 57). Somersaults, large arm gesticulations, staccato movements - some of his movements can be imitated or echoed occasionally by the revellers.

5) Simple vocabulary throughout (still imaginary glass holding for first section) - Try:
       bobbing up and down
       marching on the spot
       and stepping combinations – e.g.
(i)   step touch, step touch, stamp stamp stamp

(ii) step touch step touch step together, step touch

(iii) stamp toe heel, stamp toe heel
          l   r

(iv) step turn step together step

Chorus I

[Hey Hey Hey Hey] - three row leapfrog (C3, 60) *or* partners one behind the other - one arm out to the side, the other one up (C8, 16a) and alternate:

	Hey	Hey	Hey	Hey
person in front	out	up	out	up
person behind	up	out	up	out

or Four rows A B C & D - row at a time canon turn into the next row on each 'Hey' (C3, 53)

or Four groups - jumps in canon - particularly effective jump for this - (C3, 9) *or* heel clipping step.

The four 'Heys' happen twice every chorus in quick succession - probably effective to repeat the vocabulary each time).

If partner work in chorus try fast spiral turns (C3, 55).

Maybe baskets if time (C3, 56) whilst circles are happening at other places on stage.

Chase - little runs (skips probably too slow).

Circles - gallops or runs.

Body noise to add to the energy and raucous spirit.

Verse II

(See section on illustrative gesture)

Formed close group could also perform sequence of slapping thighs and feet plus bend and rise repetition during illustrative gesture to mark the 'umpa' rhythm in the music.

[One two three four] - Invitation for canon - maybe arms stretched out in a Buddah effect - four people standing behind each other (C4, 16d).

[Got You!]

If idea adopted of formal close group USL and distant chase DSR - the latter could enhance the interest of contrast between the two groups by performing lifts/supports on 'Got You' whilst the back group maintain an absence of physical contact (C7, 28). If only one couple chasing in this verse they could finish on table with a lift (o.k. for woman to lift man e.g. C4, 9a or 9d).

Verse III

Vocabulary is mainly composed of illustrative gesture - in close static group or groups. If levelled clump is used, devise unison directional torso sequence (e.g. torso moving side side forward back forward side, back side forward side - syncopated of course!)

Chorus II

As chorus I.

Final position:

1) Men hold two women - one on each knee (C4, 13c)

2) Some dancers in supports whilst others in overlap positions raising their glasses (C3, 71).

Potiphar from Act I, 'Joseph and the Amazing Technicolor Dreamcoat' by Tim Rice & Andrew Lloyd Webber

Choreographic Method I - Design/Vocabulary Division

The design and use of space for each section is planned *before* the vocabulary rather like painting a picture and colouring it in afterwards. With this method the design may need to be adapted or changed when the movements and steps are chosen as indeed vocabulary should in no way be subservient to design. The choreographer here has by and large outlined various alternatives for each section. Each of these will be tried out in rehearsal to decide which is the most effective.

Comments about this method. Some people find the design/vocabulary division unhelpful and prefer instead to plan the two simultaneously. Laying out possible alternatives in pre-planning notes is particularly useful for a choreographer who tends not to see new possibilities or adaptations of what he has set, when he is actually in the rehearsal room.

The Choreography Plan

Initial Reactions and Thoughts about Choreographic Needs

1. This is a nineteen-twenties number set in

Egypt! Think about the blend of Egyptian movements with twenties steps. If chorus members lack previous dance experience it is probably more sensible to do the number in a more 'Egyptian' than 'twenties' style. (There is nothing worse than a lot of poorly danced 'Charleston'!)

2. *Music* - The chorus music is given the instruction 'poco a poco accel'. Clearly the choreography for this should also get gradually faster and faster. The musical pattern is

(i)   verse
(ii)   chorus
(iii) verse
(iv)   chorus
(v)   instrumental break (same tune as verse)
(vi)   chorus
(vii) two line solo - narrator
(viii) two line solo - Potiphar

The verses are in 4/4, the chorus 2/2. 2/2 lends itself well to jumps and bobbing up and down. 4/4 will be more appropriate for the Charleston and Egyptian stepping patterns. The verse/chorus repeat will suit a choreographic repeat, possibly keeping the same steps with variation in spatial design.

3. *Set* - The set is simply a large pyramid at the back of the stage with steps running up the sides and front. The top of the pyramid can be used as the bedroom. The steps will be very useful for level variation. There may well be problems with visual competition, for example when Potiphar is in his room, Mrs. Potiphar and Joseph in the bedroom and the chorus around the stage. The pyramid steps will be useful here.

4. The correct balance at each stage needs to be decided, between the focus and the chorus and the focus on the main characters. Also a decision needs to be made as to whether the two chorus women are to be parts of Mrs. Potiphar's personality or to remain as separate personalities, or even to fluctuate between the two.

The Lyrics

Verse I (Potiphar and his Wealth)

Potiphar had very few cares
He was one of Egypt's millionaires
Having made a fortune buying shares
In pyramids.
Potiphar had made a huge pile
Owned a large percentage of the Nile
Meant that he could really live in style
And he did.

Chorus I (Joseph's Popularity)

Joseph was an unimportant
Slave who found he liked his master
Consequently worked much harder
Even with devotion.
Potiphar could see that Joseph
Was a cut above the av'-rage
Made him leader of his household
Maximum promotion.

Verse II (Description of Mrs. Potiphar and her Attitude to Men)

Potiphar was cool and so fine,
　　　But his wife would never toe the line,
It's all there in chapter thirty-nine
Of Genesis.
She was beautiful and evil.
Saw a lot of men against his will
He would have to tell her that she still was his.

Chorus II (Mrs. Potipher's Attention on Joseph)

Joseph's looks and handsome figure,
Had attracted her attention,
Ev'ry morning she would beckon
Come and lie with me, love.
Joseph wanted to resist her
Till one day she proved too eager
Joseph cried in vain, 'Please stop!'
I don't believe in free love'.

Instrumental pause

Chorus III (Potiphar's Discovery)

Potiphar was counting shekels
In his den below the bedroom
When he heard a mighty rumpus
Clattering above him.
Suddenly he knew his riches
Couldn't buy him what he wanted
Gold would never make him happy
If she didn't love him.

Narrator (Potiphar's Rage)

Letting out a mighty roar,
Potiphar burst through the door.

Potiphar

Joseph, I'll see you rot in jail
The things you have done are beyond the pale.

General Sequence of Events and Basic Choreographic Structure

1. *Verse I. Potiphar and his Wealth*
Entrance of Potiphar being carried across the stage.
   Other chorus members dance in unison to introduce twenties/Eyptian style.

2. *Chorus I. Joseph's Popularity*
Meeting between Joseph and Potiphar.
   Chorus focus on these two individuals.
   Accelerating tempo in the music, so capture the sense of speed in the steps.

3. *Verse II. Description of Mrs. Potiphar and her Attitude to Men*
Mrs. Potiphar and her two women servants show seductive attention towards the six chorus men and Joseph. Men are stationary, women moving amongst them. Use supports and lifts.
   Potiphar looking at them from the bedroom.

4. *Chorus II. Mrs. Potiphar's attention on Joseph*
Joseph tries to resist the advances of the three women.
   Two co-existing groups - (a) male chorus, (b) Joseph and the three women.

5. *Instrumental Break*
Dance by male chorus. Repeat of twenties/Egyptian steps and body designs used in Verse I. Joseph being persuaded up the steps to the bedroom by the three women.

6. *Chorus III. Potiphar's Discovery*
Potiphar sits at the bottom of the pyramid counting shekels. Panic scene between Mrs. Potiphar and Joseph in the bedroom.
   Chorus dance up the stairs to watch the action, then return to dance on the stage to avoid falling objects.

7. *Narrator's and Potiphar's Solos. (Potiphar's Rage)*
Potiphar throws Joseph into jail - which is formed by the male chorus at the base of the pyramid.

Spatial Design

Verse I. Potiphar and his Wealth

Options

(i)   Four men, one of whom is Joseph, enter carrying Potiphar. They move on a strong diagonal line USR to DSL or USL to DSR.
      The three other chorus men and the three women, one of whom is Mrs. Potiphar, form a sextet and dance around the procession (C6, 1).

(ii) The sextet dances around the carriers and Potiphar, who form a wedge shape (C5, 12).

(iii) The sextet form an equidistant group using all of the floor space, facing sideways, (C5, 19) whilst Potiphar and the carriers enter and remain in the corner of the stage DSL or DSR.

Chorus I. Joseph's Popularity

Options

(i)   Chorus (six men, two women) and Mrs. Potiphar stand in line USC facing front. At times alternate members change places sideways (C6, 10). Joseph and Potiphar mime their mutual respect DSL.

(ii) Chorus form close line facing sideways, leaning back (C5, 23). Joseph and Potiphar stand as in (i).

(iii) Chorus form equidistant unison group using the whole stage. At times Joseph and Potiphar break off from their mime to join in with the dance.

(iv) Chorus form a semi-circle around Joseph and Potiphar, having a framing effect (C7, 15; C6, 21). The back two of the semi-circle could stand on the lower steps of the pyramid to add level.

(v)   Chorus form various clusters, Joseph and Potiphar standing on the pyramid.

(vi) Chorus form one levelled clump - hands on shoulders (C3, 22). If this is too static - Joseph and Potiphar could use travelling steps and a lot of space to provide energy.

Experiment with options (i) to (vi) using one or more.
Devise suitable transitions in rehearsal.

Verse II. Description of Mrs. Potiphar and her Attitude to Men

Options

Group of Men

(i)   Men form static little groups. Experiment with variation in number, direction, and distance between group members. (See C3, 51; C7, 17; C7, 19; C7, 20; C7, 21)

or   Try USR - 2 men
       CSL - 3 men (2 men and Joseph)
       DSR - 1 man
       DSL - 1 man (a little behind man DSR).
       Adjust for perfect positioning in rehearsal.

(ii) Men form unison group standing sideways on to audience, then change to front on.

(iii) If too static, men could use more space in second part of verse, on [She was beautiful and evil]. Try crossing floor patterns with turns (C8, 24a; C8, 21).

(iv) Possible ending for [that she was still his] - men (not Joseph) run up the pyramid steps.

Group of Women

(i)   Women pass through the men from USC to DSC with
      (a) winding pathway or
      (b) straight pathway (C9, 4).
      Potiphar walks to the top of the pyramid and looks down from the bedroom.

Chorus II

Options

(i)   All 6 men walk down the front steps of the pyramid.

(ii) 4 men walk down between the other 2 men, who stand on either side like Egyptian statues (C2, 15)

(iii) Men walking down the steps can start as a close group then gradually spread out during their descent (C5, 11)

(iv) The men each choose a different step to stand on - possibly arranging themselves as a levelled wedge, e.g. 1 man on the first step, 2 on the next, 3 at the back. They then stay on the same step moving sideways. Try cannoning to either side (C9, 15).

(v)   Instead of using the pyramid, men can stay on the ground in either
      (a) diagonal a line USR whilst the seduction scene takes place DSL (C7, 26)
or (b) as a formal group USR, in contrast to the informal seduction group DSL (C7, 28)

(vi) Joseph and 3 women stay DSL with short side to side pathways. In their seduction game, women may imitate Joseph's pathway (C2, 1b).

Instrumental Break (15 bars of 4/4 - 60 beats).

Options

(i)   Unison group (6 chorus men, 2 chorus women) equidistant spacing. Use all floor space.

(ii) Close group with back lean (C3, 18a) or with more space (C3, 18b).

and/or

(iii) Use crossings (if too static)
      (a) curving crossing (C8, 18a)
      (b) diagonal crossing (C8, 27a)
      (c) side to side crossing (C8, 21)
      (d) up-stage to down-stage crossing (C8, 22)
      (e) 'dosy-do' crossing.

(iv) Joseph is pursued by Mrs. Potiphar up the steps to the bedroom.
      Potiphar, blind to this event, storms down the steps on the opposite side of the pyramid.

Potiphar's Discovery

(i)   6 men and 2 women divide and stalk up both sides of the pyramid. Mrs. Potiphar and Joseph are in the bedroom.
      Mr. Potiphar is below them, counting shekels.
      On [clattering] - duvet, cushions, pillows, flower pots all tumble down the pyramid.
      Men and women rush down the steps to avoid the barrage and run to the front of the stage.

(ii) On [suddenly] men move in a circular travelling clump, (keep facing front) (C5, 10)

(iii) Men move as a clump with a zigzag pathway (C5, 37)

(iv) Men rush manically on their own - all over the floor.

(v) On [suddenly] Potiphar stalks up the side steps, on [love him] he bursts through the door and freezes.

Potiphar's Rage

On [jail] Potiphar throws Joseph into jail from the bedroom. If it is too high, Potiphar pushes Joseph down the stairs. With the momentum from his fall he 'rolls' into the jail.
Enter Man DSL to put huge lock on the door. (Hang on one of the man's arms).

Vocabulary

Verse I. Potiphar and his Wealth

4 men carry Potiphar as if he is lying on a couch (C4, 16g). The sextet, 3 men and 3 women, dance in unison.

Options

Steps

(i) The carriers and the unison group use the same stepping combinations:
(a) step touch step touch step together step touch
and/or
(b) step together step touch step step
(crossing)
step touch.

(ii) The first combination can be adapted as a Charleston step i.e. step R forward L touches in front, step L back, R touches behind etc.

(iii) Stepping combinations could alternate with syncopated bobbing up and down on the spot. An example of 'syncopated bobbing' is:

Lyrics	He	was	one	of	Eg	ypt's	mill	ion	airs
Bobbing	up	down	down	up	down	up	up	up	down

(If two 'ups are together, the second 'up' is

higher than the first. If two 'downs' are together, the second 'down' is lower than the first.)

(iv) Group members can 'bob' at different times and/or at different levels (C5, 17a, 17b).

(v) Try alternating between bobbing and stepping at different places during the verse, and for different lengths of time.

Body Designs

(vi) During 'stepping' and 'bobbing' try the following body designs:
(a) C3, 17
(b) C3, 28a and 28b
(c) C3, 43b   *Use one or*
(d) C4, 21 (farthest right, top row)   *more*
(e) C5, 22   *of these*
(f) C5, 28
(g) C6, 15
(h) C7, 17 - using the arms of the standing group
and/or
(vii) Use the classic Egyptian stance as the main motif for the whole dance (C3, 24).

Gestures

During stepping and bobbing the sextet could use either (a) no gestures or (b) syncopated literal 'twenties' gestures, e.g.:
(i) puffing cigarettes using very long cigarette holders
(ii) twisting cuff links
(iii) straightening collars
(iv) smoothing hair
(v) head turning from side to side.

Chorus I

Steps and Body Designs

Options

(i) If syncopated bobbing was not used in Verse I, use it here,
or
(ii) use jumps for each syllable, therefore by the end of the chorus the jumps are very small!
If line is chosen, try alternate members jumping then bending.

(iii) If the sideways facing line is chosen, (C5, 23) repeat previous stepping pattern getting faster, or use a fast Charleston step.

(iv) If levelled clump is chosen, experiment with torso moving in different directions (possibly with syncopation) e.g. forward-side/back-side/forward-back/side-side.

(v) If (i) to (iv) seem too stark, add body designs suggested for Verse I.

Gestures

Options

(vi) Try including illustrative gesture on the words:
[worked] - run fast on the spot and/or mop brow.
[devotion] - bow with arms and/or kiss both your hands.
[above] - hand held high (break at the wrist like a submarine)
[maximum] - show with arms wide (break at the wrist).
    After each such gesture return to chosen movements immediately, e.g. if levelled clump is chosen, go straight back to hands on shoulders.

(vii) Ask Potiphar and Joseph to plan their own mime. Tidy it up in rehearsal. At the end Joseph may jump into Potiphar's arms.

Verse II. Description of Mrs. Potiphar and her Attitude to Men

Steps/Body Designs

(i) Men use previous stepping combinations or bobbings.
Face sideways, but with head facing front. some may sit - just tapping out the rhythm with their feet.
Exploit main motif - Egyptian stance.

(ii) The three women move with Charleston steps. Occasionally one or all women stop for support or lift with a man. They literally throw themselves at the men. Try the following supports:
(a) C4, 2d, 2e
(b) C4, 3a

(c) C4, 4a, 4b
(d) C4, 5c
(e) C4, 9a, 9d
(f) C4, 16b, 16e
and/or
(iii) On [Genesis] all women spin with a man in a turning lift (C4, 11b)
and/or
(iv) At some stage try overlapping positions - women behind men - (LC3, 64). Men without women adopt the same pose.

Gestures

(i) Exploit one previously used word gesture, e.g. cigarette blowing gesture. Men use this exclusively throughout this verse. (Try this with Egyptian stance and side to side stepping combination).

(ii) Break stepping pattern to illustrate the words:
(a) [beautiful] - show shape of woman's body and/or trace back of hand along face outline,
(b) [evil] - spikey hands and tongue stuck out.

(iii) On [that she was still his] - all chorus and Mrs. Potiphar turn to Potiphar in the bedroom as he shakes his fist at them. By this time women have frozen in a support in men's arms (C4, 3a; C4, 3b; C4, 4a; C4, 9a)

Chorus II

Steps and Body Design

(i) Men use stepping combinations to syncopate up and down the pyramid steps. Try rhythmic pattern:
    5 steps down, 1 up, 2 down, 4 up

(ii) Unsyncopated, try 1 pyramid step for each syllable, e.g.:

Jo / seph's / looks / and / hand- / some / fig- / ure
down / down / down / up / down / up / down / down

had / at- / trac- / ted / her / at- / ten / tion
down / up / up / up / up / up / up / down

If this proves impossible at the end, due to music tempo, move up or down a pyramid step every two syllables. Start this on [Joseph wanted to resist her].

(iii) Stay on the same pyramid step for the quick tempo and do side steps, e.g.:

Jo-/ seph / want-/ ed / to / re- / sist/
left / together/ right / together/ left / together/ left /

her / till / one / day / etc
together/ left / together/ right/

(iv) Use simple body designs for this, maybe simply hand on hip, head forward (C5, 29), or slight back lean, one arm forward (C3, 23a).

(v) Joseph and three women move DSL. Three women form a line and lean towards Joseph as he leans away, (C6, 15). Use quick steps. *Or,* Joseph and Mrs. Potiphar (C3, 19) alternate between advancing and retreating towards and from each other, whilst other two women freeze in seductive poses.

(vi) At the end each woman places a hand on Joseph's body, ending in position C3, 7. One hand on each beat:

Lyric   'till one day she proved too eager
Hands 1   2   3   4   5   6 7 8

(The first woman has to do the last two hands.)

(vii) On [Joseph cried in vain 'Please stop'], Joseph throws women's arms off him. All women freeze with their hands over faces looking aghast, whilst Joseph sings, [I don't believe in free love].

5. Instrumental Break (fifteen bars of 4/4 - 60 beats

(i) Use this as a chance to reinforce earlier vocabulary. Use earlier stepping combinations, body designs and gestures (see Verse I for all of these).

If this seems to be too repetitive, use the ones not tried before.

(ii) Add canon to start and finish. Try random canon (C9, 10d) and three small group canon (C9, 13, 14).

(iii) Mrs. Potiphar pursues Joseph who goes up the steps backwards on his bottom. She wafts him with a giant fan up to the bedroom.

6. Potiphar's Discovery

Steps and Body Design

(i) Men and women stalk up steps with similar 'up down' pattern as before (but with the emphasis on travelling up rather than down!)

Exaggerate stalking with forward leaning body design and huge arm movements.

(ii) On [suddenly] if circular travelling clump has been chosen for the chorus, use tiny little steps.

(iii) If manic rushing has been chosen, use lots of jumps, rolls, bumpings to add to the chaos.

Freeze on the word [him] in levelled random group (C3, 31).

(iv) Gestures for the Chorus
Use illustrative gesture whilst stepping on the words:
[counting] - counting
[below] - point finger (whole body involvement) at Potiphar
[clattering] - hands vibrating over ears, head rolling round and round very fast.
Repeat hands vibrating during the section [suddenly] to [love him].

(v) Main Characters
Mrs. Potiphar and Joseph have a polite rhythmic row in the bedroom. She tries to hug him with syncopated rhythm. He ducks (see C4, 19b). Adapt this, using a hug instead of a hit.

On [love him] Mrs. Potiphar throws herself into Joseph's arms (C4, 6c) and freezes.

(vi) Potiphar's stalking starts on [suddenly] with big, exaggerated creeping steps, one step for each syllable. 16 steps are needed to arrive at the top by the word [him]. If not enough pyramid steps, do a 'step together' on each pyramid step (8 pyramid steps are needed), or step every two syllables. On [him] Potiphar throws open the bedroom door.

7. Potiphar's Rage

(i) Chorus kneels, hands over ears vibrating,

and/or lie flat on the floor, legs vibrating in the air (C3, 63) (from [Letting] to [rot]).

(ii) Chorus form jail on [rot].
Make square, backs to centre with arms linked in military stance.

(iii) Joseph stands in jail, arms stretched up to the heavens, head thrown back in despair.

Bingo Song (Music 15) Act II 'Beowulf' by Ken Pickering & Keith Cole

Choreographic Method II - The Table

The choreographer sets out on only one page in table form his ideas under headings 'general activity', 'design/formation', 'illustrative gesture' and 'specific vocabulary'. There are no alternaives planned and no line by line instructions.

Comment. The value of this method is that the choreographer can easily see the overall shape of the number. It is also very effective in rehearsal as it avoids the usual flicking through pages to find the next instruction. It is obviously inexact and would not suit the choreographer who cannot think of new steps and designs spontaneously in the rehearsal room. However it is well suited to the choreographer who prefers only to outline ideas in pre-plannning stages and to leave spatial transitions, exact spacing and movement combinations to the rehearsal. Hopefully in rehearsal such choreographic details will develop naturally out of the few movements which have been pre-planned and taught.

The Choreography Plan

Initial Reactions and Thoughts about Choreographic Needs

1. Think of ways of avoiding visual competition between Mrs Grendel, the hostesses and the old ladies, e.g.:

a) Mother can attract attention by speech; old ladies and hostesses by movement.

b) There probably will not be much competition between old ladies and hostesses, as hostesses are directly behind old ladies but higher up, there being no problem of merger or interference, therefore, due to difference in level. Hostesses could even at times act as a frame for old ladies, but be careful hostesses are not too high up on scaffolding otherwise they may go unnoticed. Try to have hostesses' feet sometimes just above ladies' heads, therefore no break for the eye. Hostesses may need more lights if competition with Mrs Grendel and ladies is too great.

c) Have moments of stillness at different times in each of the three groups so spectator can sometimes just focus on one group.

d) There may be competition between Mrs Grendel and old ladies. Think carefully where to put her in relation to them. Sometimes she could enter their semi-circle.

e) Sometimes Mrs. Grendel, hostesses, old ladies can all perform identical movements in unison to show their connection and, therefore, this can give the eye a rest for a time.

2. See costume designer. She hasn't decided on colour of material yet. It would be nice to have different plain, but complementary colours for each group, with possibly some matching item, e.g. hostesses' waistbands, old ladies' handbags, and Mrs Grendel's shawl, all made of the same colour material.

3. Decide whether to use bingo boards or not.

4. All involved in events of the song, so very little front on movement, apart from the hostesses.

5. Think of how to arrange the semi-circle of chairs. Try out alternatives so all ladies can be clearly seen. Ask stage manager if chairs are round backed, square backed, folded and if they have foot rungs, before choreographing chair movements.

6. Think about ways of incorporating visual humour in terms of vocabulary and spacing, e.g:

a) Visual contradiction - beautiful hostesses next to clumsy old ladies.

b) Imitation, mimicking of old ladies by hostesses.

c) Idiosyncratic gesture plus personal body contact for the old ladies.

d) Fast tempo and acceleration movements getting out of control - throwing chairs and boards about.

Music 15: Bingo Song

Mrs. Grendel (singing)

On the red, Hrothgar's fate
Thirty-eight.
On the blue, Danish wench
Twenty-two
But what's this on the green
Hrogarth's Queen - seventeen
Oh yes one day soon I'll smash her little skull.
On the red, devil's hive
Nine till five
On the green Grendel's tricks
Fifty-six.
On the blue, well look you
Thatcher's den, number ten
Yes, she and I are really quite good pals
On the blue, doing fine
Sixty-nine
Still on blue number two
Sutton Hoo.
On the green sweet sixteen
Viking swine number nine
Oh dear how I hate that nasty little lot.
On the blue, death to you, eighty-two.
Hate, hate, hate, number eight on the red
Number three, look at me can't you see what
                                    I've got
Oh, I've a certain something they have not.

She chants into the mike in an even more frenzied way until, by the end of the song she is completeley berserk

On the red stay in bed, sixty five
On the green, quite untouched, just thirteen
Savage Picts, twenty-six, black and blue forty
                                        two.
And so now we really start to move it by

(Faster still)

Number three, now bad luck always comes
Like the wolf at the door forty-four.
Ninety-nine, now you're mine
Forty-three don't you see
I hate your Anglo-Saxon poetry.

Now eyes down on the blue thirty-two
Rape and crime do your time twenty-nine
On the make forty-eight, on the blue,
                                    twenty-two
Why we must all make profit from the state.

During the following Beowulf swims in - preferably from above down a huge strand of water weed.

King of tricks, politics, sixty-six
Take a dive on a bribe, ninety-five.
Forty-one, twenty-eight, human kind going
                                    straight
I hate oh how I hate yes HATEY HATE!

THE BINGO SONG

	General Activity	Design/Formation	Illustrative gesture	Specific Vocabulary
OLD LADIES	Sitting on chairs, holding bingo boards (C11, 4), comparing, cheating, hitting each other with hand bags. Getting up, sitting down, changing places, bobbing up and down. (Usually identical movement either in unison or canon - otherwise visually confusing with hostesses and mother dancing on stage as well).	Semi-circle of chairs - old ladies stay in this formation although they may change places and grovel on the floor on occasions	Join in with Mrs Grendel's illustrative gesture for *Smash her little skull* *Death to You* *Eyes Down* - possibly stand up for these. *But what's this* - ladies express surprise, shock, hand vibrations in air and legs out to the side in air. *Take a dive* - all dive on the floor - one of them has dropped a handbag - all grovel around to steal contents.	1. Wiggling, shaking, swaying, pulsating, in chairs. 2. Torso leans (see C3, 18c, 28a, 29) - but sitting down not standing up. 3. Personal body contact - e.g. scratching heads, hands on chin (C3, 15a, & 28b), hands over eyes, C4, 20b, pulling up stockings (for more examples see C4, 21). 4. Head isolations, shoulder isolations, (C3, 30). 5. Lying or standing on chairs (C10, 13). 6. Bobbing up and down (C5, 17a, b, c). 7. Syncopated phrases and ripple canon of movements where appropriate.
(Mrs Grendel) MOTHER	Gestures as sings, gets aggressive with the microphone, adjusts her 'beautiful' dress. Joins in with some of the	Paces up and down at the side of the semi-circle of old ladies - sometimes enters the semi-circle - or climbs onto the	*Smash her little skull* - hand action as if crushing an egg and watching the contents trickle to the floor, then wiping hand	Hand gesturing often to show strength of emotion and hate - leave this to rehearsal - but ideas of clenching fist or opening

	General Activity	Design/Formation	Illustrative gesture	Specific Vocabulary
	movements of hostesses and old ladies - but sometimes moving in double tempo to show how she is getting out of control. She is clearly competing with the hostesses in terms of sexiness. She holds a microphone in one hand, therefore only has one hand free for gesture and movement.	scaffolding with the hostesses, often deliberately to upstage them. Keep floor patterns short and infrequent -otherwise too much visual competition for others on stage.	*clean on dress (all in quick syncopated phrase).* *Eyes down* - Grotesque finger point - head movement follows the air pattern of the finger. *Death to You* - hand around own neck and head and torso circling movement. *Hate Hate Hate* - Three fist waggles with three little flat-footed jumps. Join in with Mother's gestures for: *Smash her little skull* *Death to You* *Eyes Down*	hand quickly, or throwing arm out violently to the side. Imitating movements of other two groups at times.
HOSTESSES	Sexy dancing, always on the scaffolding. Waving around prizes at times perhaps (C10, 4). Taking off head-dresses - using feather boas (C6, 14). Dancing with the scaffolding poles, sometimes hanging around or off them (C10, 20). Joining in with old ladies, bobbing up and down, and Mrs Grendel's gestures sometimes.	Lots of lines with close proximity and physical contact (e.g. C4, 2e). An 'overlap' line facing front (C3, 67). Lines facing side or back. In pairs overlap and complementary shapes, Buddah effects (C4, 16a & d). Mostly four together - sometimes two plus two - no three plus one - keep it symmetrical.		Torso leans in line(C5, 23, 25, 28). Flat torsos facing side (C6, 8 & 7). Back arm up in line (C5, 28). Cat steps (C3, 11). Simple arm actions - repeated (C3, 50). Join in with old ladies - personal body contact and idiosyncratic gesture sometimes - imitation mimickry - but doing it sexily. Finish - surrounding Mother - hands covering her body (C3, 7).

'Oklahoma' Finale Number from 'Oklahoma' by Richard Rodgers & Oscar Hammerstein II

Choreographic Method III - Sectioning of Events

The number is divided into four clear sections: 1) gesture section; 2) male/female ensemble; 3) partner work; 4) unison formation work. Design and vocabulary are integrated in each section. Some alternatives are given.

Comment. A very clear and efficient way to work in the rehearsal room. The danger is that this somewhat crude division and dis-section of the piece could result in a choreography which lacks unity and is seen as four unrelated sections by the spectator. With this method the choreographer needs to think carefully about the transition from one section to the next. It can help if there is some main movement theme running throughout all four sections.

The Choreography Plan

Initial Reactions and Thoughts about Choreographic Needs

1. Incorporate women's full skirts in some of the movements.

2. Formal groupings with order, balance and equidistance seem appropriate for this production number.

3. Use a lot of 'front on' movement, as it is a finale, direct unambiguous communication of energy with the audience must be at its highest.

4. Male/female ensembles and different reactions of the sexes to the same events will help to emphasise the underlying theme of marriage. The song is very 'couple conscious'. This is an open invitation for double work.

5. Frequent spatial transitions, and formation changes, as well as lots of jumps will help to generate the necessary energy level.

6. Travelling energetic movement is inappropriate in the opening slower section I. The main aim here is to establish the closeness of the family group outside their house.

7. Few of the lyrics lend themselves to illustrative gesture.

8. Note the increase in tempo in the repeat of the refrain and the general feeling of crescendo. Parallel these in the choreography.

9. High points are [Oklahoma] and [Yeeow!] - mass reactions. Note these.

10. Avoid complex vocabulary as there are a lot of people and it is appropriate for a finale such as this. Simplicity spatially and in terms of vocabulary will lend itself more to spectacle here.

OKLAHOMA LYRICS
Section I (50 beats)

They couldn't pick a better time to start in Life
It ain't too early and it ain't too late
Starting as a farmer with a brand new wife
Soon be living in a brand new state
Brand new state! Brand new state!
Gonna treat you great!
Gonna give you barley, carrots and pertaters
Pasture for the cattle, spinach and
                                    ter-may-ters!
Flowers on the prairie where the June bugs
                                    zoom
Plen'-y of air and plen'-y of room
Plen'y of room to swing a rope!
Plen'y of heart and plen'-y of hope

Refrain
Section II (16 beats)

Oklahoma, where the wind comes sweepin'
                                    down the plain
And the wav-in' wheat can sure smell sweet
When the wind ocmes right behind the rain!

Section III (16 beats)

Oklahoma, every night my honey lamb and I
Sit alone and talk, and watch a hawk, makin'
                                    lazy circles in the sky

Section IV (24 beats)

We know we belong to the land -
And the land we belong to is grand!
- And when we say - Yeeow!
A-yip-i-o-ee-ay! -
We're only say-in' you're do-in' fine
Oklahoma - O.K.

Oklahoma

General Sequence of Events (Four Sections)

Section I. Lyrics [They couldn't pick a . . . →
plen'y of hope]

   Gesture section - Close group on terrace.

Section II. Lyrics [Oklahoma . . . → behind
the rain]

   Male/female ensemble.

Section III. Lyrics [Oklahoma . . . → circles in
the sky]

   Partner work.

Section VI. Lyrics [We know we belong . . . →
Oklahoma O.K.]

   Unison, Formation work.

Section I. (No. of beats: 50)

1. All on the terrace in front of house - family
and friends. Main couple Laurie and Curly in
centre at top of five steps on terrace which
lead down to rest of stage. Rail on terrace -
soloist singers lean on it, sit on it, jump over
it. Clump - semi-circular with level variation.
Half way through clump move down steps -
some sit on them, others stay on terrace.
Some couples are distinguishable here - in
identical overlapping positions (C3, 60). Finish
this section by all moving as a clump DSC.

2. Soloist singers very little actual illustrative
gesture but [Plen'-y of room to swing a rope]
- soloist here can make a big swinging rope
action - group reaction - chorus duck out of
the way. Soloists can use hand actions to
demonstrate the emotional energy behind their
statements (don't pre-set these - design what
comes naturally to soloists in rehearsal). Don't
overdo group reactions to soloists' statements.
This is a fairly static section - but nods to
neighbours, leans towards singers, arm round
a neighbour's shoulders, 'involved' faces are
all appropriate. (Ask dancers to improvise
these ideas in rehearsal and then set what
comes out of this).

Section II. (No. of beats: 16) Male/Female
Ensemble

Start (four beats - instrumental to run into
position) in male/female group - male group
USL, female group DSR (C5, 16). Laurie and
Curly DSL. Curly sings to Laurie throughout
this section, one arm round her, gesturing
with the other arm, e.g:

[Sweep-in' down the plain] - extended arm
sweep looking behind the audience.

[And the wav-in' wheat] - small to and fro
gesture with the hand.

[When the wind comes right behind the rain]
- gentle lowering of gesturing arm. Laurie
stands and looks up at his face.

They stay on the same spot.

[O---k-lahoma] (4 beats)
Women - 4 spins arms in upturned 'V'
Men   - Hands in braces - 3 step touches
          (r, l, r) one jump, hitting knees with
          both hands in the air.

[Where the wind comes sweep-in' down the
plain] (4 beats)
Women - 4 pas de basque steps (l, r, l, r) -
          swishing skirt in figure of eight each
          time
Men   - 4 heel clipping jumps (l, r, l, r)
Next 8 beats:
[And the wav-in' wheat can sure smell sweet
When the wind comes right behind the rain]

Groups crossing in 2 arcs with 5 gallops -
women hands on skirts, men hands on waist
(4 beats) (C8, 24b). Man grabs lady on the
last beat i.e. [rain] and whole cast move into a
formal distant group with partner (C5, 5)

Section III . (No. of beats: 16) Partner Work

[Oklahoma] - hand on waist turn together
(C3, 55) - free hand in the air. On the 'k' of
Oklahoma both stand facing front and lower
outside arm slowly with other arm still round
partner's waist.

[Every night my honey lamb and I] (4 beats)
Half the cast stay in position - men perform
turning lift with women (either C4, 11a or 11b
or 11e) or turn women over (C4, 10b). The
men in the other half of the cast move (little
runs) to form a diagonal line at the side of the
stage (try out other positions for this in
rehearsal - maybe on the terrace). Their
women form two clumps, one at each end of
the line.

[Sit alone and talk and watch a hawk, (8 beats)
Makin' lazy circles in the sky].

The line of men spin one woman down from one end to the other (C6, 9).

The two clumps of women sway and sing.

The other half of the cast remain in their same positions, each man kneels (one knee). Women kick leg over their partner's head with a turn and sit on partner's knee, arriving by the word [watch]. Women in unison then make a circular gesture in the air on [lazy circles].

Laurie and Curly during this section have moved DSL as far as possible so as to be clearly separate from the rest of the action, but they join in with the chorus by Laurie sitting on Curly's knee and performing the women's circular gesture on [Makin' lazy circles etc.]

Section IV. (No. of beats: 24) Unison, Formation Work

[We know we belong to the land] (4 beats)
8 gallops crossing (C8, 21) into formation - spread out (C5, 5). Alternate man/woman/ man/ woman, 4 on each line (C6, 4). Women perform quick up and down movement with skirts during gallops with a torso lean forward. Men slapping thighs during gallops with a torso lean forward.

[And the land we belong to is grand! - And when we say . . .] (6 beats)
Try 1) heel clicking jumps (4 beats)
    2) leg kicking pas de basque steps (4 beats)
    3) 4 jumps kicks (legs high in front - r, l, r,l,)
On [and when we say] 2 spins, arms in high 'V' [Yeeow!] (2 beats) low position - bent knees - arms to side, open palms as in C3, 15b - but legs crossed not apart.

[A-yip-	i-o-	ee-	ay]
V	V	V	V
Group A	Group B	Group C	Group D

(5 beats)
Canon movement - one arm into air, very straight torso, feet together, head to the ceiling.

The canon employs a hidden structure for grouping as in C8, 10 (but four groups).

[We're only say-in' you're do-in' fine Oklahoma - Ok-la-homa - O.K.] (8 beats)

Try (with gallops or little runs or skips, or pas de basque steps):
1) changing places in lines (C6.10)
2) front facing dosy do
or turns/spins in canon, one line moving into the next and back (C2, 53) i.e.
Line A → Line B → Line C → Line D → Line C → Line B → Line A

Final Position

Try 1) Variation in set levels and body levels with different groups (C5, 21)

    2) Three groups - all different positions (C3, 39)

    3) Hidden structure - sudden drop of some dancers, with same position but lower on last note (C8, 9; C4, 10)

    4) Some partner work, supports and lifts, whilst other cast members remain separate (C3, 71).

Repeat of the Refrain

Do not pre-plan this - either run through all four sections again or extend the Section IV so that the group stay in the unison 'distant' formation for the whole of the repeat (may need more complex vocabulary for the repeat if this choice is opted for).

Notes for Rehearsal

a) If unison Section IV is too crowded, make two or three side static singing clusters (C7, 25).

b) If any section is too rushed, leave one until the repeat of the refrain, so as to allow the other sections more time.

'Light of the World' and preceding dialogue - end number in Act I, Godspell by Stephen Schwartz

Choreographic Method IV - Line by Line Planning with Floor Patterns

A method where movements and use of space are devised simultaneously and are described in detail for each line of lyrics verbally through instruction and visually with floor plan diagrams.

Comment. The method is very thorough and so makes it easy to pre-visualise the complete choreography plan and decide whether it will work or not. It is suited to those choreographers who do not tend to get inspired in the rehearsal room and who therefore prefer that every minor detail is pre-set before meeting the dancers. For other choreographers this method is over rigid and lacks the flexibility of a method such as 'The Table' (illustrated in the 'Bingo Song'). If this method is employed, the choreographer should be careful not to 'over-cater' in terms of design, spatial transitions and specific movements. In other words it is a common fault to cram in too many ideas into one phrase of music. Therefore when the choreographer comes to try out his plan on the dancers he finds there is not enough music for each movement phrase and the choreography looks ridiculously rushed. However it is easy to rectify this by merely omitting some of the pre-planned movement instructions and floor plans and making others last twice as long as the time originally allocated to them on paper.

Note about Floor Plans. With this way of working, it is advisable to 'stock up' with a whole wad of empty floor plans on which to scribble down ideas. Simply photostat several pages of them (see page 150). The format used is adapted from the original 'Laban' idea.

Key

O— indicates the dancer and the direction he faces to start with. There is then a gap and his stopping place is indicated by →. Thus in the next floor plan O— is put in place of the →.

LIGHT OF THE WORLD

Stephen (in rhythm)
Is there a man among you who will offer his son a stone when he asks for bread?

All (milling centre in rhythm)
Is there a man among you who will offer his son a stone when he asks for bread?

Stephen   A snake if he asks for fish?

All   No

Stephen   Well if you now/Bad as you are/ Now, know how to give your children what is good for them/ How much more will your heavenly Father give good things . . .

All   Good things!/Good things!/Good things!/Good things!/Good things!/ Yeah!

Stephen   . . . to those who ask for them/ Always treat others/As you would have them treat you/

All   Yeah/yeah/yeah!
(moving to positions for 'Light of the World'

Stephen   Well, that is the law and the prophets.

All   The law and the prophets
The law and the prophets
The law and the prophets
The law and the prophets
The law and the prophets
The law and the prophets
The law and the prophets

Music Cue: Light of the World

Herb   You are the light of the world

All   You are the light of the world.

Herb   But if that light's under a bushel It's lost something kind of crucial

All   You've gotta stay bright To be the light of the world

Peggy   You are the salt of the earth.

All   You are the salt of the earth.

Peggy   But if that salt has lost its flavor It ain't got much in its favor.

All	You can't have that fault and be the salt of the earth
	So let your light so shine before men
	Let your light so shine
	So that they might know some kindness again
	We all need help to feel fine.
David	Let's have some wine!
Jeffrey	You are the City of God
All	You are the City of God.
Jeffrey	But if that city's on a hill
	It's kind of hard to hide it well
All	You've gotta stay pretty in the City of God
	So let your light so shine before men
	Let your light so shine
	So that they might know some kindness again
	We all need help to feel fine (Let's have some wine!)
Robin	You are the light of the world.
All	You are the light of the world.
Robin	But the tallest candlestick
	Ain't much good without a wick
All	You've gotta live right to be the light of the world.
	So let your light so shine before men
	Let your light so shine
	So that they might know some kindness again
	We all need help to feel fine
	Let's have some wine!

The Choreography Plan

Initial Reactions and Thoughts about Choreographic Needs

1. Not much space as the set limits the dancing area, but the small amount of space does allow for quick formation changes.

2. One could use the set (cyclone fence enclosure nine feet high and open on the audience side - sits on a bare stage) for soloists to climb on, hang off.

3. Group members are involved with each other, therefore not much front on activity.

4. Informal group, therefore avoid formal equidistant grouping. Organised chaos and random grouping will be appropriate at times.

5. The Refrain is repeated three times - would possibly suit choreographic repetition - in other words 'ABC BDB' structure.

6. It is an emotionally close group thus physical contact is appropriate - particularly whole group body buildings (e.g. the human heap or human chair (C4, 18b).

7. Remember it is a cast of 10 - nine plus Jesus (Stephen) - some possible combinations:
3+3+3+1/4+5+1/3+3+2+1+1/2+2+3+1+1+1/
4+2+2+1+1

8. Probably more appropriate to start preplanning from the music rather than the lyrics in terms of choreographic 'clues', clearly illustrative gesture not really appropriate.

9. Points to note from the music:

a) Very clear rhythm 4/4 slow rock - lends itself to clapping and slow torso movements as opposed to fast intricate stepping combinations.

b) There is an instrumental break in four of the solo singing sections (chord + 3 beat break, chord + 3 beat break). These may sometimes lend themselves to a movement freeze or pose. The breaks are not long enough for a choreographic virtuoso section (not like a tacit section in a tap dance). Possibly use the chords to make a transition from one movement freeze to the next. The breaks may be observed by just the soloist, just the chorus or both simultaneously - decide this.

c) It seems important to adhere choreographically to the crescendo sign under [Let's have some wine].

d) The refrain is 32 beats long and the change of mood in the music would allow for this to be choreographed with fluid and frequent spatial transitions and formation change.

Godspell Floor Plans
Please note: Stephen (Jesus) is represented
in the floor plans by a black circle •

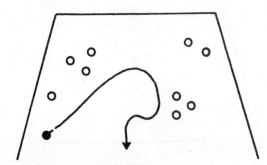

Floor plan 1

Lyrics (complete section)
Note: Stephen is Jesus.

Stephen*   Is there a man among you who
           will offer his son a stone when he
           asks for bread? (8 beats).

All   Is there a man among you who
           will offer his son a stone when he
           asks for bread? (8 beats)

Breakdown of Lyrics:

Stephen   [Is there a man among you who
           will offer his son a stone when . . .]
           Stephen runs in big sweeping curve,
           bent knees, outstretched 'accusing'
           arm and finger. (Rest of cast freeze
           on varying levels)
           [he asks for]
           Stephen fast turn to right (cross left
           leg over right) [bread] - Stephen
           breaking bread action with hands,
           to audience.

All   (8 beats) [Is there a man among
           you who will offer his son a stone
           when . . .]
           All + Stephen free asking gestures
           to people/person close to them.
           [he asks for]
           All - fast turn to right (cross left leg
           over right)
           [bread?]
           All - breaking bread actions with
           hands to audience.

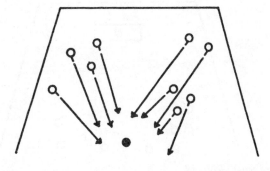

Floor Plan 2
Lyrics
Stephen   (4 beats) [A snake if he asks for
           fish?]
           Stephen stands motionless. Cast -
           run run run step leap to Stephen.

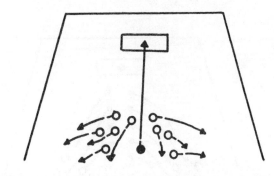

Floor Plan 3
Lyrics
All   [No!] Cast fall to knees, heads and
           arms thrown back. Stephen pushes
           them all out of his way.

Stephen   (4 beats) [Well if you now/Bad as
           you are . . .]
           Cast roll out to sides of stage.
           Stephen walks backwards to set
           with step bounce click step. He
           jumps onto the set on word [are].

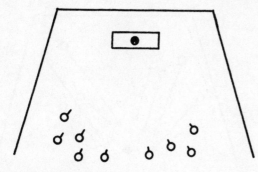

Floor Plan 4

Stephen   (10 beats) [Now you know how to give your children what is good for them/How much more will your heavenly father . . .]

Stephen hangs on to set with one arm, gesticulates with other. Cast turn to face him and kneel.

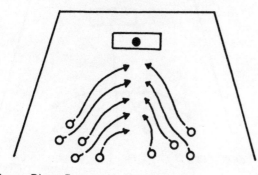

Floor Plan 5

Lyrics

Stephen   (2 beats)[. . . give good things . . .]

Cast run to Stephen and form double line

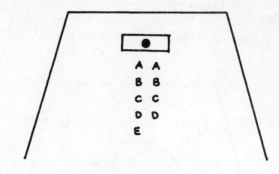

Floor Plan 6a

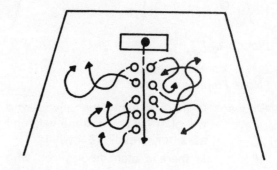

Floor Plan 6b

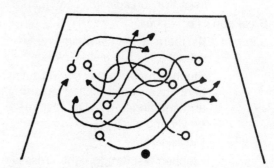

Floor Plan 7

Lyrics   (5 beats)   [Good things!/Good things!/Good things/Good things!/ Good things! Yeah!

Stephen walks down stage. As he passes each couple in turn they spin out in canon, scattering to the sides of the stage. (Therefore one couple spins on every [Good things]. One person must spin on his own). Then all jump around - organised chaos (work out exact floor patterns here in rehearsal). All - quick freeze on the 'h' of [Yeah] in three groups (see Floor Plan 8)

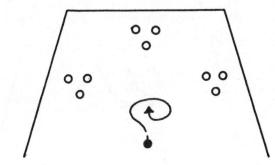

Floor Plan 8(a)

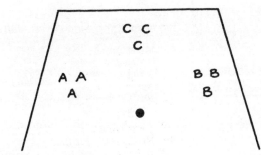

Floor Plan 8(b)

Lyrics

Stephen   (7 beats) *(Group A):* [to those who ask for them]
(Group B): [Always treat others]
(Group C): [As you would have them treat you]

Stephen walks round as in Floor Plan 1 - smaller circle, one phrase addressed to each of the three groups (see above). Cast - freeze with a variety of level and body contacts (e.g. supports, or leans - but casual)

All   (3 beats canon - see Floor Plan 8(b))
[Yeah] - Group A - arms up in air - outstretched fingers vibrating
[Yeah] - Group B - arms out to side - outstretched fingers vibrating
[Yeah] - Group C - bend knees, arms lower - outstretched fingers vibrating

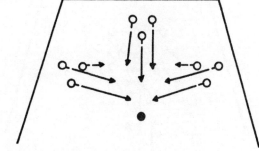

Floor Plan 9(a)
Lyrics

Stephen   (3 beats) [Well that is the law and the prophets]

Cast freeze. Stephen on word [that] starts step touch step touch and finger click and moves arms as in (C3, 17) + head isolation - relaxed feel.

All   (2 beats) [The law and the prophets]
(2 beats) [The law and the prophets]

Cast move towards Stephen - step touch, step touch × 2 coming forwards - arms (C3, 17) + head isolation.

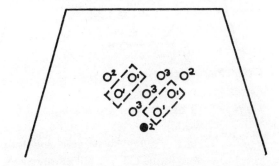

Floor Plan 9(b) (6 beats)
Lyrics

[The law and the prophets] - 'ringed' people drop to the floor and bounce/others clap
[The law and the prophets] - people marked '2' drop to the floor and bounce
[The law and the prophets] - people marked '3' drop to the floor and bounce. All stand together on 'ets' of proph*ets*

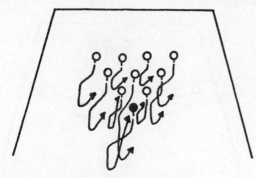

Floor Plan 10 (4 beats each)

Lyrics

All   [The law and the prophets] -
[The law and the prophets] -

All follow Stephen's floor pattern with little runs (one foot to the other). Arms by sides. On 'ets' of proph*ets* Herb moves DSC

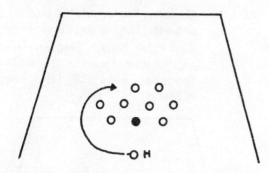

Floor Plan 11(a)

Lyrics

Herb   (8 beats) [You are the light of the world]

Herb - sway sway step together step (arms C3, 17). All - sway sway step turn step (arms by sides)

All   (8 beats) [You are the light of the world]

All join in with Herb to repeat his sway sway step together step (arms C3, 17)

Herb   (4 beats) [But if that light's under a bushel]

Herb (H in diagram) moves to the back line and hides behind person in front of him (C4, 16a). All cast freeze as different statues

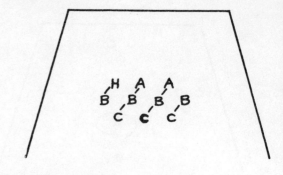

Floor Plan 11(b)

Lyrics

All   (6 beats)
[It's lost something *kind of crucial*]

As hide behind Bs and freeze in position (C4, 16e)	Bs hide behind Cs and freeze in position (C4, 16e)	Cs hide behind someone imaginary! (C4, 16e)

All jump up straight on 'I' of cruci*al* *(2 feet to 2 feet jump)*

All   *(4 beats)*[You've got to stay bright]

All 'square' (see stepping combinations)

All   (4 beats) [To be the light of the world]

All step turn, step, turning jump - finish (C3, 17)

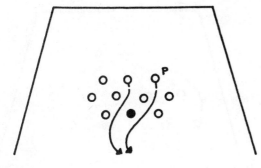

Floor Plan 12(a)

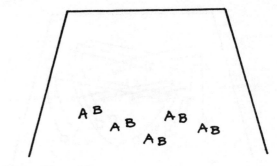

Floor Plan 14

Lyrics

All   (8 beats) [You are the salt of the earth]

All keep up step bounce, clap (l then r) then on [earth] all spin into a partner's arms.

Peggy   (8 beats) [But if that salt has lost its flavor/It ain't got much in its favor]

On word [salt] Peggy's partner lifts her (C4, 9a)

On word [favor] Peggy's partner throws her into the air before she lands.

(Cast freezing in partners' arms during this)

All   (8 beats) [You can't have fault and be the salt of the earth]

All repeat Peggy's left and throw on words [fault] and [salt] in couples.

Peggy and partner sing side by side during this (no gestures)

(Start of Refrain)

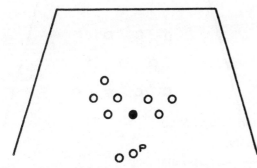

Floor Plan 12(b)

Lyrics

Peggy   (8 beats) [You are the salt of the earth]

Peggy skips through the group taking another member of the cast with her. All step bounce clap on the spot. On word [earth] Peggy spins into her partner's arms (C4, 6c). She freezes.

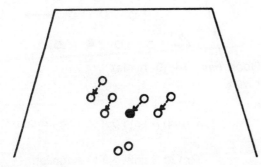

Floor Plan 13

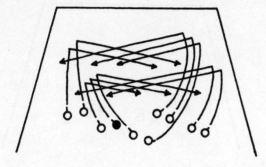

Floor Plan 15(a)

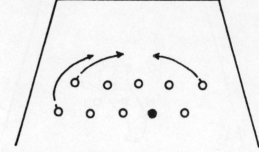

Floor Plan 17(a)

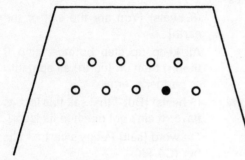

Floor Plan 15(b)

Refrain

All   (8 beats) [So let your light shine before men]

Group split into two, run up sides of stage and cross through each other - finish in two lines (8 runs)

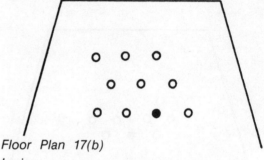

Floor Plan 17(b)
Lyrics

All   [So that they . . .]

Three members spin to make a three line formation

All   (8 beats) [might know kindness again]

Torso leans - syncopated (unison) (C3, 23b). Two to the right, one to the left, one to the right. On [kindness] open arms slowly to the side and straighten torso.

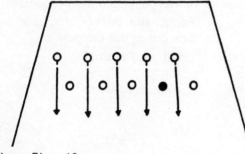

Floor Plan 16
Refrain

All   (8 beats) [Let your light so shine]

Back line travels forward through gaps in front line. Try three runs and a leap *or* walk r, l, r kick ball
                         (l)

change and kick touch to the side
     (r)   (l)

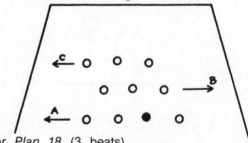

Floor Plan 18 (3 beats)
Lyrics

All   [We . . .]

Group A spin out to stage right
[all . . .]

Group B spin out to stage left
[need help . . .]

Group C spin out to stage right

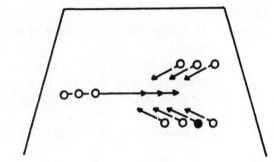

Floor Plan 19(a)

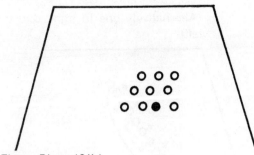

Floor Plan 19(b)

Lyrics

David   (5 beats) [To feel fine . . .]
             [Let's have some wine]

             All run into middle of stage, leap
             and end in C8, 6 - different levels,
             arms out and flickering hands.

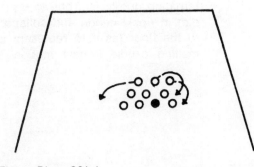

Floor Plan 20(a)

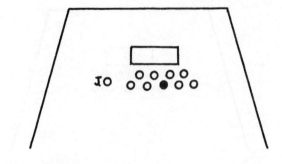

Floor Plan 20(b)

             Group drop into two lines, Jeffrey
             moving farthest position in the
             group - stage right.

Lyrics

Jeffrey   (8 beats) [You are the city of God]

All   (8 beats) [You are the city of God]

             All in unison repeat torso move-
             ments + C3, 17 +C3, 48a step touch
             bounces.

             (Assemble this in rehearsal in terms
             of too much or not enough repe-
             tition of main movements

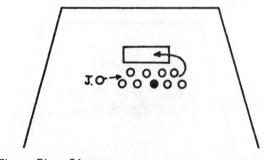

Floor Plan 21

Lyrics   (4 beats)

Jeffrey   [But if that city's on a hill . . .]
             Jeffrey's
             4 steps: 2 31 4   up
             human steps (body building C4,
             7d) - to represent the hill

Jeffrey   (4 beats) [It's kind of hard to hide
             it well]

             Jeffrey jumps on set - middle of
             the stage

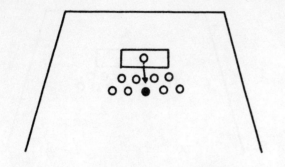

Floor Plan 22 (8 beats)

Lyrics

All   (8 beats) [You've gotta stay . . .]

Cast move to be on either side of Jeffrey

All   [pretty in the city of God]

Jeffrey jumps off set into arms of the group (C4, 13a). Arms in a 'V'. Stephen (Jesus) kneels in front of Jeffrey - back to the audience - in a complementary shape (arms in same position as Jeffrey)

Refrain - repeat Floor Plans 15 - 19b

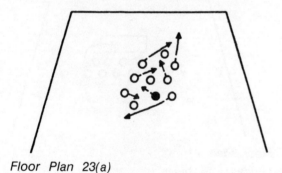

Floor Plan 23(a)

Lyrics

Robin   (8 beats) [You are the light of the world]

All form diagonal line. Perform syncopated torso movement (C5, 23) forward, back forward + head isolation to the side

All   (8 beats) [You are the light of the world]

Repeat of syncopated torso tilts (C3, 23b) - finish (C3, 17)

(Alternatively one to right, one to left)

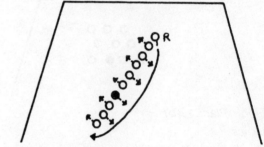

Floor Plan 24

Lyrics

Robin   (8 beats) [But the tallest candlestick Ain't much good without a wick]

Robin walks down the line - as he passes each person they turn (alternating one to left, one to right, etc) in ripple canon and collapse to the floor (as if to represent a melting candle in fast motion!)

Floor Plan 23(b)

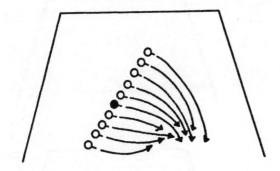

Floor Plan 25(a)

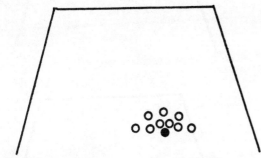

Floor Plan 26(b)

Lyrics

All   (8 beats) [You gotta live right to be the light of the world]

All run into clump DSC to start the refrain. Middle two people lift Stephen as they go (C4, 9c - but one person on each arm)

Finish in C4, 16g - Stephen lying across five people who then kneel with him.

Other four people stand behind in position, C3, 17.

Refrain   See Floor Plans 15 - 19.

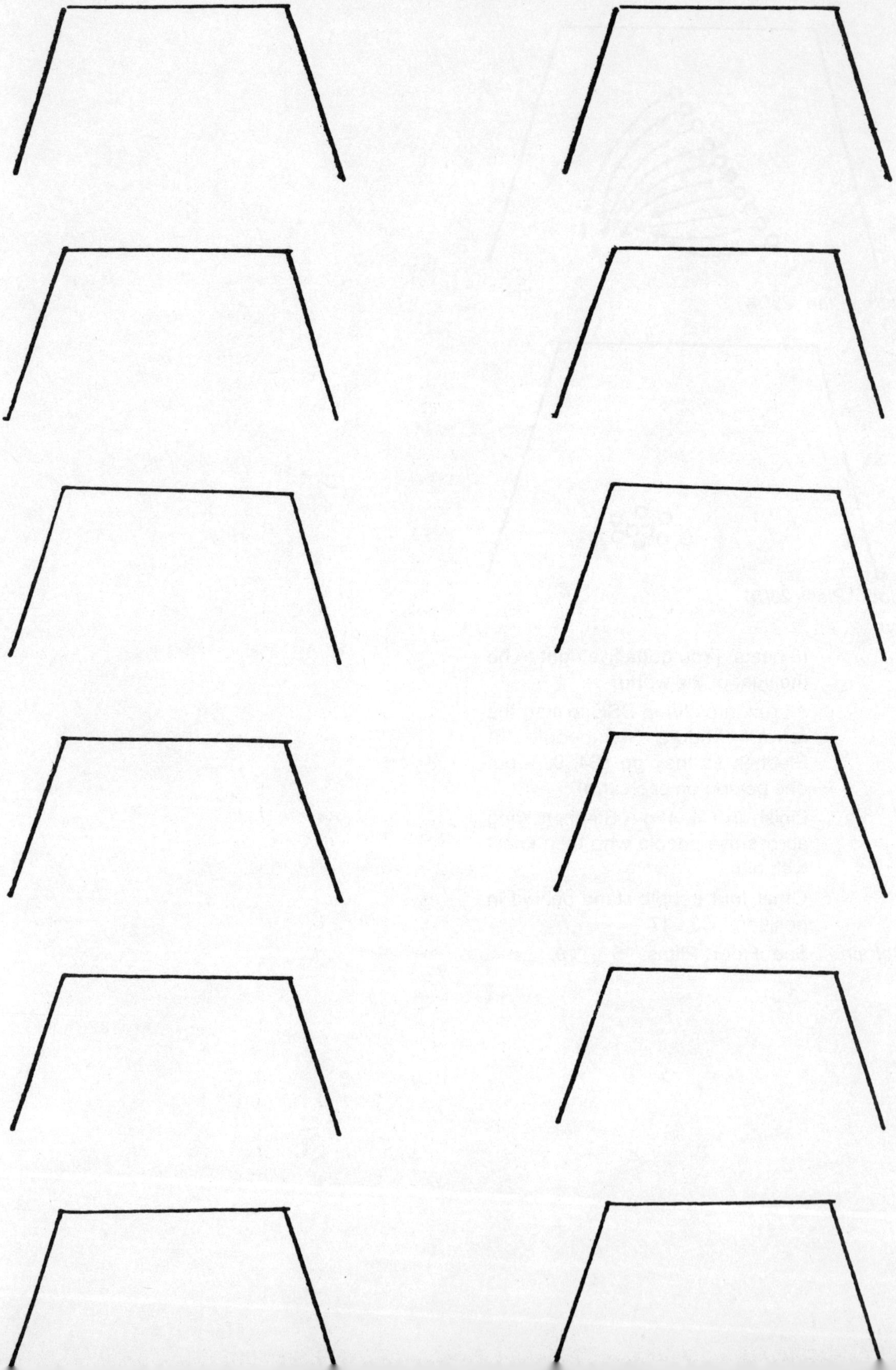

Appendix II

MUSICALS REFERED TO WITHIN THE TEXT

American in Paris, An
Books & Lyrics, Arthur Freed. Music, George
Gershwin.

Annie
Book, Thomas Meehan. Lyrics, Martin Charnin.
Music, Charles Strouse.

Applause
Book, Betty Camden & Adolph Green. Lyrics,
Lee Adams. Music, Charles Strouse.

Bandwagon
Book, Betty Camden & Adolph Green. Lyrics,
Howard Dietz. Music, Arthur Schwartz.

Beowulf
Book & Lyrics, Ken Pickering. Music, Keith
Cole.

Boyfriend, The
Book, Lyrics & Music, Sandy Wilson.

Cabaret
Book, Joe Masteroff. Lyrics, Fred Ebb. Music,
John Kander.

Call Me Madam
Book, Howard Lindsay & Russel Crouse. Lyrics
& Music, Irving Berlin.

Camelot
Book & Lyrics, Alan Jay Lerner. Music,
Frederick Loewe.

Carousel
Book & Lyrics, Oscar Hammerstein. Music,
Richard Rodgers.

Dazzle
Book & Lyrics, John Gardiner. Music, Andrew
Parr.

Dracula Spectacular
Book & Lyrics, John Gardiner. Music, Andrew
Parr.

Easter Parade
Book & Lyrics, Arthur Freed. Music, Irving
Berlin.

Evita
Book & Lyrics, Tim Rice. Music, Andrew Lloyd
Webber.

Fiddler on the Roof, A
Book, Joseph Stein. Lyrics, Sheldon Harnick.
Music, Jerry Book.

Flying Down to Rio
Book & Lyrics, Gus Kahn & Vincent Youmans.
Music, Irving Berlin.

42nd Street
Book & Lyrics, Rian James & James Seymour.
Music, Harry Akst.

*Funny Thing Happened on the Way to the
Forum, A*
Book, Burt Shevelove & Larry Gelbart. Music &
Lyrics, Stephen Sondheim.

Godspell
Book, Lyrics & Music, Stephen Schwartz.

Good Companions, The
Book, J. B. Priestley. Music, André Previn
Lyrics, Jonny Mercer.

Grease
Book, Lyrics & Music, Jim Jacobs & Warren
Casey.

Guys & Dolls
Book, Jo Swerling & Abe Burrows. Music &
Lyrics, Frank Loesser.

Gypsy
Book, Arthur Laurents. Lyrics, Stephen Sondheim. Music, Julie Styne.

Hair
Book & Lyrics, Gerome Ragni & James Rado.
Music, Galt MacDermot.

Half a Sixpence
Book, Beverley Cross. Lyrics & Music, David Heneker.

Hello Dolly
Book, Michael Stewart. Lyrics & Music, Jerry Hermann.

How to Succeed in Business Without Really Trying
Book, Abe Burrows, Jack Weinstock & Willie Gilbert. Lyrics & Music, Frank Loesser.

Jesus Christ Superstar
Book & Lyrics, Tim Rice. Music, Andrew Lloyd Webber.

King and I, The
Book & Lyrics, Oscar Hammerstein. Music, Richard Rodgers.

Kiss Me Kate
Book, Sam & Bella Spewack. Lyrics & Music, Cole Porter.

Little Night Music, A
Book, Hugh Wheeler. Lyrics & Music, Stephen Sondheim.

Match Girls, The
Book & Lyrics, Bill Owen. Music, Tony Russell.

Mothers and Daughters
Book & Lyrics, Ken Pickering. Music, Keith Cole.

My Fair Lady
Book & Lyrics, Alan Jay Lerner. Music, Frederick Loewe.

New York, New York
Book, Earl Macrouch. Lyrics, John Kander. Music, Fred Ebb.

No, No Nanette
Book & Lyrics, Oscar Hammerstein. Music, Richard Rodgers.

Oliver
Book, Lyrics & Music, Lionel Bart.

Pirates of Penzance, The
Book & Lyrics, W. S. Gilbert. Music, Arthur Sullivan.

Seven Brides for Seven Brothers
Book & Lyrics, Albert Hackett & Frances Goodrick. Music, Gene De Paul & Johnny Mercer.

Singing in the Rain
Book, Betty Comden & Adolph Green. Lyrics, Arthur Freed. Music, Nacio Herb Braun.

Smike
Book, Lyrics & Music, Oscar Hammerstein. Music, Richard Rodgers.

Sound of Music
Book & Lyrics, Oscar Hammerstein. Music, Richard Rodgers.

South Pacific
Book & Lyrics, Oscar Hammerstein. Music, Richard Rodgers.

Sweeny Todd
Book, Hugh Wheeler. Lyrics & Music, Stephen Sondheim.

Sweeny Todd Shock 'n' Roll Show, The
Book & Lyrics, Randall Lewton. Music, Peter Miller.

Sweet Charity
Book, Neil Simon. Lyrics, Dorothy Fields. Music, Cy Coleman.

Top Hat
Book, Lyrics & Music, Irving Berlin.

Ulysees
Book & Lyrics, Ken Pickering. Music, Keith Cole.

West Side Story
Book, Arthur Laurents. Lyrics, Stephen Sondheim. Music, Leonard Bernstein.